MW01001567

A Mother and Daughter Dialogue across the Veil

ANDREA COUREY

Author photo credit: asbed.com
Cover photo credit: Andrea Courey

Balboa Press books may be ordered through booksellers or by contacting:

Balboa Press
A Division of Hay House
1663 Liberty Drive
Bloomington, IN 47403
www.balboapress.com
1 (877) 407-4847

Print information available on the last page.

ISBN: 978-1-5043-7239-8 (sc)
ISBN: 978-1-5043-7240-4 (e)

Library of Congress Control Number: 2016921283

Balboa Press rev. date: 02/14/2017

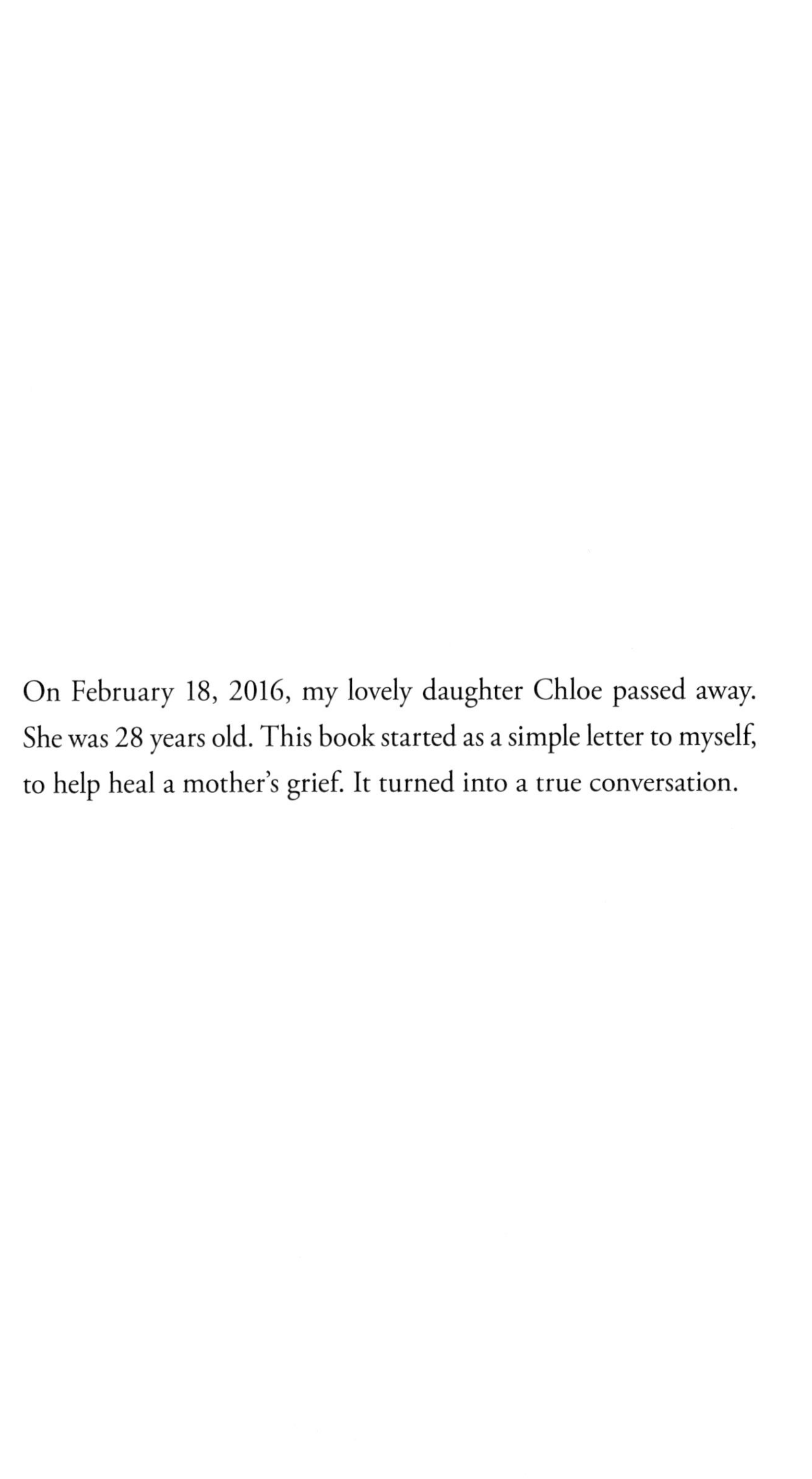

On February 18, 2016, my lovely daughter Chloe passed away. She was 28 years old. This book started as a simple letter to myself, to help heal a mother's grief. It turned into a true conversation.

DEDICATION

To all mothers trying to cope with the loss of a child.

FOREWORD

Andrea Courey is one of those rare people who energize any room or conversation. You'd never guess the life behind that upbeat, ingratiating and inspiring personality has been anything but easy.

A single parent with three children to care for when her nine-year marriage collapsed, she started a small granola business in the kitchen of her home in Montreal, and with determination and industry turned it into a viable enterprise that she eventually sold.

That's how our paths first crossed. As a reporter covering small business for the Montreal Gazette newspaper, I was intrigued by her venture and her career path. My initial interview with her, in 1999, on the steps of her small commercial kitchen, was one of the most memorable I can recall in over 40 years in journalism.

She was frank, she was funny, she was spontaneous and unpretentious, a fount of imagination and empathy and compassion and curiosity. The interview included a self-deprecating quote that still today is one of my all-time favourites: "One of my friends told me I'd be on Oprah someday. I said 'I hope it's not the show where she interviews bagladies'."

We kept in touch after that, curious about the directions each of our lives were taking.

I thought I knew her pretty well, but it turns out there was a lot more to her story than she'd ever revealed to me.

This book, inspired by the loss to colon cancer of her daughter Chloe and a way of channeling the life experience from it into something enduring and far-reaching, fills in the spaces.

Unfailingly honest, often poetic, it takes the form of an exchange, through imagined letters rooted in real events, between a mother and her departed daughter over some of the choices, conflicts, omissions, joys and life lessons of their respective journeys, changed forever by Chloe's death at 28.

True as always to her optimistic nature, Andrea finds beauty, inspiration, dignity and peace in an emotionally wrenching twist of fate that takes a beloved child far too early and shakes, transforms and takes over her own life at age 54, just when she'd finally begun living fully on her own terms.

Unexpectedly, the shared ordeal and final separation brings them closer.

She comes out of it with a determination to "push the reset button" and start life anew, guided by a clearer understanding of herself, the legacy of a daughter whose short and troubled life was, in its own compelling way, a blessing.

As Andrea puts it, "when the worst possible thing happens, and you survive, you come out the other side realizing it wasn't the worst thing. It was, in fact, a gift."

—Paul Delean

CHAPTER 1

Letter to Chloe

Hi, Clo. It's April 1, 2016. You would love this place. It would be your ideal spot, just beside the lake. The geese glide by, and I've been told there are beavers, but I haven't seen any yet. The ice is still jamming the banks. Things move fast around here—I mean things like water and ice. One minute, the chunks are all bunched up, jostling for position; the next minute, the lake is clear.

You would love my wood-burning stove. It's small but powerful, and it heats my whole space with a furious crackling, threatening to bust out beyond the grill. It's not difficult because my whole space consists of one room, about 400 square feet.

I never would have searched to rent in this area if I hadn't taken a leisurely drive along Lakeshore Road that wintery January day. I wouldn't have taken the leisurely drive if I hadn't been out in that neck of the woods. I wouldn't have been in that neck of the woods if I hadn't accepted an invitation to speak at the university's Faculty of Agriculture, which is out this way, on Wednesday, January 20, at 3:00 p.m. I almost backed out because it was the same day you went into palliative care at the hospital.

I did honour the commitment, and I spoke about my favourite topics: entrepreneurship, single motherhood and how to survive it all. As I left the campus, I knew it would be a long night at the hospital, so I decided to wend my way back unrushed, slowly driving the 30-kilometer speed limit along the winding road that hugs the lake for miles. It brought me peace.

It was almost 11:00 p.m. when I got back to my parents' home from the hospital, and I began searching Airbnb for somewhere to live. Not having a home of my own hadn't bothered me until now. When I'd sold my home a couple of years ago and left to experience life in another part of the country, I'd been happy to have no possessions, with nothing tethering me to anywhere. Now I realize that's not possible. Our past always calls us back. And back I came—to love and care for you.

I knew your death was close, and I felt the need to stay close to home. I wanted a place to hang my hat, a place to help me heal, a place close to loved ones and close to water. At 11:05, I found this tiny cottage on the shore of a large lake. It was 20 minutes to downtown, 20 minutes to family and friends, and 20 feet from the water's edge. The lake is four to five kilometres wide in front of the cottage and is clean, full of fish, and swimmable. The farmers' market, the pharmacy and the grocery store are just minutes away by foot; so are the train and bus into the city.

One email exchange, and it was secured for the whole summer.

The owner of the property, John, lives in the big house 30 feet away. Both homes are tucked away from the street, face the lake and are surrounded by mature trees and gardens. Years ago, John had used this cottage as his office. Imagine that kind of commute to work—50 paces and you're there! If I had been able to envision a place to live, and if I'd had the ability to imagine such a country setting only minutes from the downtown core, I would have imagined this.

My precious 400-square-foot space contains a queen-sized bed at one end with two small night tables on either side; a simple, two-and-a-half-foot by four-foot table along a window that functions as my kitchen; a love seat; a solid-wood, round table with two wooden Windsor chairs; and the crowning glory of the place, my wood-burning stove. The "kitchen" consists of a two-burner hot plate, a toaster oven and a mini-fridge. That's it. The bathroom is literally my washroom. All washing—dishes, clothes and self—happens in there.

I love it.

The first thing I did when I arrived was remove all the blinds. John rolled his eyes, commenting that other tenants had complained of too much light in the morning. Imagine, Clo—is there such a thing as too much light?

I have no complaints.

John came for dinner the first two nights. I knocked myself out creating gourmet meals with my two little burners. The firelight and candlelight provided the rest. I struggled—successfully, I might add—to keep my hands to myself. The atmosphere was thick, heavy and dripping romantic. You've gotta understand, we've been communicating for two months non-stop—emails, texts, FaceTime, phone calls. Barriers came down so quickly. I had fallen for him long before we actually met.

He's at home now, mercifully. I glance out the window and see the firelight dancing on his ceiling. I know where he sits: always on the same sofa, in the same spot. It's nice to know he's there, yet I like being here on my own. It gives me the space to grieve in private whenever I want to. And right now, I want to.

I'm 55 years old and living in one small room. No more possessions, no job, and no Chloe. I'm on the floor, moaning. Grief takes me deeply into my body. It overwhelms, suffocates, rumbles through me like an earthquake that shakes and shakes and threatens to bring the house down. Only there's no house. There's just one human being trying to cope. Physical, sharp, real pain in the centre of my being. The grief is deeply physical. Already it's been six weeks since you've been gone.

On the other hand, here I am, 55 years old, and I can finally rest in peace. Your suffering is done. Thank God. What an ordeal for you and for all of us. It's over. You can continue, live, grow and explore. I can sit in my small studio with its magnificent, large view and begin to heal.

I feel you nearby. I just glanced out the window, and night has fallen, hard and dark. When did that happen? My new world is slow. The quick pace of outside things continues to startle me. Moments ago, I was watching the ice crowd and toss; now, only the flickering lights of the seaway are discernible. There's nowhere to go. No one needs me. It's like learning to walk again. I remember I used to do this, used to have my own life, but I'm not quite sure where this new life is going.

I remember years ago, arriving at my office—we called it the kitchen. I'd arrive really early, leave late and realize that I hadn't felt the sun on my face for even one blessed moment that day. That made me sad. It was part of the tough sacrifices of trying to raise the three of you and run a business at the same time.

Now I have time to sit with my face to the sun as spring begins to unfold in this beautiful spot. I have the time to notice how the clouds scurry across the sky, and the fact that the birdsong begins long before sunrise (the first robin sang at 4:22 this morning), and how the wind blows. A growing habit of mine is to determine the wind direction every day, and to extrapolate the coming weather. Today, it's a south-westerly breeze of about 12 knots. If it's an easterly wind, I expect stormy weather tomorrow. John, a lifelong sailor, talks about the wind a lot. I never actually thought of the wind before, except in relation to how much it would mess up my hair.

I rise early and watch the colours fill the sky long before the sunrise. When the official time of the sunrise hits, the show is already over. The bleachers are empty; the roadies are stacking the chairs, the crowd is gone and the air is silent. Not a hint of birdsong.

We have a pair of mating ducks that reside on our lawn, an elusive rabbit that seems to have taken up residence in my kayak, a muskrat that lolls around in the water camouflaging as a small log and assorted fowl and flora. We have plenty of firewood to burn. This fire is the absolute best one I ever made: loud crackle, great flame and heat. I'm tucked away from life, private, living small and yet living large at the same time. I'm up before sunrise every day, and that suits me just fine.

What defines living big? Living on purpose, living fully, not compromising, not settling. Every day, choices present themselves, and I choose. Then I honour that choice and keep going. I forgive myself because I make many less-than-stellar choices. But still, I keep choosing and dreaming big. It's like I pushed a reset button, and my life is now starting over. I'm not quite sure yet what its direction will be.

I like the idea that my new "kitchen" is just one step away from my bed. The economy of space has an aesthetic that pleases me: no waste. The freedom of frugality with no extravagance, unless you consider the sunrises and sunsets. Two glasses, two cups, two forks, two knives, two dishes—a Noah's ark of domestic simplicity.

The view from the windows was more a priority than the number of kitchen cabinets: four windows, zero cabinets. I wanted to live surrounded by beauty after so much time clocked at the hospital, as well as outside its walls, hanging out while you smoked. I needed to gaze on water and be surrounded by nature.

John mentions that he's lived here for 30 years, and he has stopped noticing the beauty. Imagine that. My daily comments about the stars, the moon and the faraway lights of the seaway that speak to me in a Morse code of adventure seem to prod him out of a learned complacency.

I've officially begun my book project. I have a smaller sideline project that also needs fulfilling. I'm in search of hugs. I can live without sex for a bit, but not without hugs. Maybe I'll enlist John.

Letter to Mom

Mom, you are so easy to find that it's a joke. Your light shines really bright. Yup, it's me, Clo. I know you're not even surprised. I know you feel me peering over your shoulder, digging my chin into you like I used to do. A weird, tender act, but a tender act nonetheless.

I really like using the word nonetheless. *When can I do that? Not often enough. I want to be a part of your book. I'm excited to do this project together. I'm excited to have a voice, a real voice, a normal voice, a voice that can be calm or get excited but is never crazy.*

It was exhausting being so crazy. The yelling and screaming, the fighting of the invasion in my head. Now, my head is clear.

Everything is clear, and the job is finished. So this is not a job, not a chore. This is fun, right?

I can feel you really need a hug. I'm going to help you find someone great to hug you. Is it okay if it's John? That's gonna be tricky, Mom. That attraction could ignite a forest fire.

I do love the place. We're a lot alike. It's easier to see that, now that I'm not totally crazy anymore.

Mom, all I really want to say is I love you. I'm so sorry I caused you so much grief. I'm sorry I never paid you back all the money I stole. I stole lots of other stuff too, from other people; I'm sorry about that too. Could you please get to the African store on Saint Laurent Boulevard, tell them I'm sorry and pay them? That'll be just more I owe you.

John? Seriously? Sit on those hands! Sit on those hands, at least for a little while. He does have incredible hands too, doesn't he? Worked, rugged, battered a bit, in need of loving—here we go.

Letter to Clo

I hear you loud and clear. I've felt you so close every day. And you're right about John: he does have incredible hands.

I wonder if you could work with an iPad? Type the letters yourself? The touch is so light.

I'll work on that.

Boy, we did a few miles, eh, Clo? I burnt a lot of gas trying to make you happy. I burnt a lot of brain cells, a lot of dollars and time and so much energy trying to find ways to make you happy. Then I finally realized I couldn't do one blessed thing to make any difference in what you were living. I just had to do the one thing I was always meant to do from the very beginning: love you. So I did.

Clo, I'm excited! I found the spot right by the water to write my book. There's even a little platform on a huge tree that juts out over the water. Once April gets into bloom, I'm going to head out on that platform and write to you. Oops, slip of the words. I mean write the book.

What's the book going to be about? About you, about life and death and about whatever else presents itself. About how it feels to write with the water and currents and wind to guide me. About how the sound of nature heals me. About boys. About those crazy, red-winged blackbirds on their spring romance campaign.

March 29, 2016 Day 1 - View from My Doorstep

There is so much to write. In fact, I already have boxes of scribbles, but they're just that: scribbles. This is going to be different, actually organized. I'm not sure exactly how, but I know the how will come, right?

I always said, "Andrea, just focus on the why. Know your why. The how will show up 400 times a day, in every phone call and meeting and choice that presents itself. The how is the universe unfolding my why."

So I'm not going to worry about how. Today is April 1, and I'm going to write this book. By July, it is done. I know that tense makes no sense, but I don't want to talk about it being done in the future. It is done *now.* Except now is going to be four months away … whatever. As long as my heart is open, words will flow.

I know how much you love words too. Here's a new one for you: *disintermediate.* As in, "getting rid of the middleman." As businesses become more transparent, this is possible in some industries.

What about, "as human beings learn to communicate with the other side, we nudge away the veil of mystery and the unknown"? We can do away with intermediaries like priests and rabbis, who have no greater connection to all things of spirit than we do. Disintermediate. That's what we're doing, Clo: we're learning to disintermediate. We don't need a psychic, a séance or a healer. We simply need to be open enough to ask, to listen and to trust.

Letter to Mom

That's my kind of word—15 letters. Anything over 12 letters is a word worth remembering—unless we're playing Scrabble. Remember when, Mom? We were great adversaries.

Because of the memorial money donated in my name, the Cedars Cancer Research Fund is going to kick-start the Pet Therapy Program. The money they collected will help people with cancer receive that special brand of love that only our animals can give us. I can do good from this side, Mom. You can't know how that helps me heal.

Remember that line from The World According to Garp*? "You gotta get obsessed and stay obsessed."*

Let me know how it goes with Matthew today.

Letter to Clo

Hi, Clo. Your brother was in good shape today. Even though I woke Matt up when I got there at 11:00 a.m., he was keen to shop for groceries, make lunch and enjoy it together.

I suggested that we make a raw salad that had one thing cooked in it; it could be vegetable or animal. He chose to marinate chicken breasts in a homemade honey mustard, cook them on the stove, slice them and add them to a salad. He shopped for all the ingredients, prepared everything and served us both. It was a true hit. Rather than search for conversation, we shopped, cooked and ate. Two hours together that were well spent, were productive and helped him regain a bit of power. Now he knows how to make a one-dish salad dinner. We have a date for next Friday at 11:00 a.m.

He complains that the medication makes him groggy and sleepy, but I know his diet has a lot to do with the lethargy that surrounds him. He's constantly yawning and rarely smiles. He has a lot of congestion. He eats a sugary cereal for breakfast and drinks a lot of soft drinks—poison!

You hardly ever smiled either. Both of you—brain cells ruined by drugs. The resulting mental illnesses completely short-circuited your lives. They threw a grenade in the middle of a family, ruined our precious home life, destroyed your promising futures, exhausted all caregivers and shrank your options of where and how to live.

With so few options for symptom reduction and regaining

quality of life, the diagnoses for both of you were harsh: if you lose your minds, you lose everything.

Almost every day, I ask myself which came first, the drugs or the mental illnesses? Which was cause, and which was effect? I have no idea. I had never even heard the word *bipolar* before Matt's meltdown.

I have a harder time dealing with Matt, who's alive, than with you. I have a harder time accepting him as he is than I had with you. This accepting thing demands acceptance that all is as it should be. How can I accept that my brilliant son—who was admitted to law school, was a top student with a promising future, was an engaged and intelligent young man with every advantage given to him—is now a schizophrenic living on social welfare? That label is permanently attached to him. There is no recovery from this illness, just management. Hopefully.

It's almost too much for a mother to bear. I'm stripped down to my naked self. No expectations or desires for anything or anyone outside myself. This includes my children. How do I let go of hopes and dreams that began the moment I knew you were in my womb? Slowly and with lots of gentleness for myself.

Sometimes I get stuck on old wants, like him getting a job or not having his hand out for money all the time. I want him to be normal, but he's not. I want him to have friends, meet a girl and have a life. But he can't. He's stuck. He talks out loud to himself while in his own world with his company of weird, imaginary friends. He laughs to himself, making strange gestures and carrying on conversations. They're real to him. I struggle with accepting his world as more real to him than this one.

I hear parents obsess about their children's grades, or the entrance exam for middle school that's coming up. I think, *Just give them a hug and tell them you love them no matter what.*

I say nothing.

Sometimes I have a vision of my heart bleeding and bleeding. The blood runs out of my chest, turning my white blouse a scarlet red. My heart literally bleeds for him. The blood strangles my voice and breath.

Matt has stacks of cards—those strange cards with wild illustrations on them. I ask him whom he plays with. He tells me there are four players at the table, him and three imaginary friends. At least he talks about it. Imagine: he's 29 and spends his days playing cards with his invisible friends.

Remember the day last September, when I shaved my head? All those long, dark, sexy locks—gone. What a relief. When asked why I did it, I realized there was no simple answer. It was my way of pulling my hair out in grief over you, over Matt, over all the losses in my life. It was a way of making myself invisible to men so that I could focus solely on you. It was also a way of being in solidarity with you and the concept of letting go. It was self-punishment and self-flagellation that helped me grieve more deeply for myself, as well as for you both. It probably was many other things too.

Even after six months of chemo, you never lost your hair, but I could see you were losing the battle. And what could I do? Driving for hours around the countryside didn't adequately express my mammoth-size grief. Shaving my head and relinquishing my identity helped.

Boy, did we ever drive! Even after months of driving, every morning you still wanted to get out of the house and hit the road. You hung your head out the window, face to the wind and eyes closed. I keep seeing that scene from *The English Patient* when they're in the plane, and she's in the seat behind him, only she's dead and we don't know that till the end.

If we could have explored other therapies—if you had been open to that—I would have tried everything and anything, from eating sprouts and a raw-food diet to checking you into the Hippocrates Health Institute in West Palm Beach for massive doses of wheatgrass juice. That was too much to wish for, so I settled for simply bringing you those two weary clichés, peace and love.

You did your utmost to try to push us away, yet you remained well surrounded. We never gave up on loving and caring for you. Came close a few times, though.

Thank you. When I was out for my run this morning, you diffused the air inside that tunnel with cigarette smoke. Because it was a small tunnel, I was easily able to smell it. Well done. Sometimes I think I smell it, but am not sure because I'm out in the open air. It was very, very smart to do it in the tunnel. Thanks, Love. I knew you were nearby.

Welcome.

Another thought: Work is truly a holy endeavour because whatever work you do, your spirit imbibes the work. If you are a carver, your spirit carves into the wood. If you are a baker, your spirit infuses that bread. If you are a granola maker, your spirit permeates that granola. That is why work is divine. That is why one must never take one's work as just a way to earn a pay cheque. Doing that negates what the purpose of work is: the expression of one's spirit in the physical world.

This book is the physical manifestation and expression of my spirit. It matters. It is authentically a reflection of who I am, the experiences I've been granted, the oneness, the aloneness, the loneliness, the joy I've lived. It's a conversation with you about death and life, about nothing and everything. It's a mother and daughter dialogue. It's an exchange between kindred spirits who recognize the grace of the other, the contribution of the other, the oneness with the other.

I need to take time with this so that I can ask you a question in my head, and then clear myself away so that I can receive your answer. I don't want to make anything up. I want to truly hear your words and transcribe them.

Another observation about my environment: Living close to the water is completely different from living in an urban environment. Here, the weather changes, and one takes note immediately. The sky is large; the water is always present. One feels the shifts in weather a lot faster. In a city with tall buildings, the weather can shift, and one doesn't even realize it because the sky is so far away. Here, the sky is ever-present. I love that. The sound of the water hitting the stone wall is my constant lullaby. Sometimes it's gentle, sometimes it's radical and sometimes it's actually scary in its pounding presence.

As I was meditating this morning to the cries of eagles and rolling waves on the tape, the red-winged blackbirds and robins were making a racket right outside my window.

Note to self: It's impossible to have the time for meditating while working, raising children and trying to have a life, so let's go easy on ourselves. Okay, ladies?

Clo, imagine this, the true story of today's events. I'm at John's house making granola, and we start kissing. It was bound to happen; the physical attraction is amazing. It's actually more than a physical attraction. I'd call it a nonphysical heart attraction that ignites a physical reaction. We spend about three hours talking, necking and making out on the couch like teenagers. Delicious.

Then I feel a shift in his energy. I look at him and ask him if he had finished with his girlfriend. He says, "Not exactly." I pull away. Five minutes later, the doorbell rings. It's her! I had felt her presence minutes before she rang the bell.

I leave out the back door, angry mostly with myself for allowing my attraction to steer me in the wrong direction—again. Another man, another deception.

I pack up my stuff and decide to leave first thing in the morning. I'm trying to avoid the melodrama, but it reeks of drama. An amazing afternoon of sharing, and then she rings the bell.

No more distractions. It's time to write.

CHAPTER 2

Letter to Mom

I'm laughing, Mom. I'm laughing so hard, watching you muddle around in this thing with John. First you create the connection electronically; links are created and reinforced through the openness that email affords. Then you meet, and the physical takes over. A man in need of kindness, gentleness and a bit of mothering meets a woman who is the ultimate mothering kind.

He: strong and delicate of heart. You: delicate and strong of heart.

I watched you pack your stuff in a fury, then unpack it in the morning.

I know exactly why you stayed in your little place. You wanted to stay close to John. You're trying to tell me it's because you paid the rent, or because you love the little cottage, or because you don't want others to think you're flighty. But the real reason is you want to stay close because you feel something you haven't felt in years: Passion with a capital P.

Your friend Sue says a lot of really smart stuff, like, "We're 95 percent brilliant and 5 percent messed up. How come we focus on the 5 percent? How come we listen when others focus on the 5 percent?"

Maybe John's 95 percent great and just 5 percent screwed up about women?

The difference between a bad haircut and a good one is three days. In other words, hang on a bit, take a few breaths and let things settle before overreacting and regretting it later.

So I've become the guide, the helper, the sage one. I can tell this absolutely delights you. The master was clothed in the body of a psychotic prostitute. How'd ya like that? Ya gotta believe, no?

I must be deaf, dumb and blind, but I'm crazy about this man. I'm keen about this project, and I need to have a bit of patience with this whole love triangle thing. I'll keep my Zen distance for a few days. And yes, I love this cottage too.

Good luck with that.

With what? Forget it—I won't ask.

John tells me he's an alcoholic. What? Hasn't had a drink in almost six years. He goes to his AA meetings every week, talks openly about his past struggles and says how wonderful he feels to have his life back. He's frank, open and direct. There's alcohol in his house for guests. He insists it's fine if I drink around him, but I'd rather not. Since I stopped drinking—my maximum was two glasses of wine a day—those bizarre stomach pains have disappeared. So have the few extra pounds I wanted to lose and the puffiness around my eyes in the morning.

I'm intrigued about the process he went through to overcome addiction, the famous 12 steps. He hands me his book covered in his scribbles, the margins full of his thoughts and observations of other members, of the process.

There's that number 12 again. Twelve apostles, 12 months, 12 steps, 12 days of Christmas. As I read the manual, I'm intrigued that the language has not been updated. It's a conscious choice to keep the text true to Bill W., the original scribe who wrote it in 1953.

Here's my quickie interpretation of the AA text. On the left is the main gist of each step. On the right are my suggested words for a new millennium.

Step 1: Admit powerlessness: Acceptance

Step 2: Believe that a higher power can help: Become conscious

Step 3: Decide to turn the problem over to God: Surrender

Step 4: Take moral inventory of self: Awareness

Step 5: Admit wrongdoings to others: Let go of the ego

Step 6: Be ready to move forward: Intention

Step 7: Ask to remove shortcomings: Humility

Step 8: Make amends to others: Atonement

Step 9: Take responsibility for one's actions: Peace of mind

Step 10: Make moral inventory a habit: Deliberate thinking

Step 11: Pray and meditate: Mindfulness

Step 12: Pay it forward: Service with gratitude

I feel like a miner, constantly digging to get at the heart of something, trying to get to the place of really knowing about something. It's like how I know about you being alive and about there being no death, just transformation. And once you know, you know.

Knowing the philosophy he follows helps you understand John better.

You're right. I really respect the demon he deals with. Not one drink in six years. Do you think it could have helped you?

I didn't want help.

In that case, step 13: Crash and burn: Allowing. That was my big learning. To allow you to be you.

Letter to Clo

I saw him naked this morning. It was actually around 6:00 or 7:00 a.m. I woke at 3:00 a.m. By 5:00, I was going absolutely out of my mind. I put on red rubber boots and my shawl and walked over. The door was unlocked. (He had told me he'd leave it unlocked.) I let myself in and surprised him a bit when I crawled into his bed. Then there were four hours of bliss.

I'll share the thought that gave me the courage to go over there. I thought, *God wants me to be happy. He wants me to thrive, to live, to laugh, to create.* Going over there and crawling into John's bed would make me really happy, so, off I went. I did get halfway there and turn back once, but the second time I went for it.

I saw him naked. Yes, he has a big belly, but the funny thing is, I'm still crazy about him. As the saying goes, he had me at hello.

Even though I was in my comfy cotton PJs in his bed, I didn't even think I should put on something sexy. We've been talking for months. He's seen me with no make-up, no fancy clothes. He's seen me in my PJs. The comfort level between us is so great that I didn't think I had to get dolled up. I simply had to show up.

I love the touch of his skin. His face is deeply lined; it is a totally imperfect face, a lived-in face, perfect in its imperfections. It's a face that has squarely taken wind, rain and sea squalls. A weathered, beaten face with much character. A face I can honestly say that I love.

I do. It's crazy, but I do.

When he sent me out the door at 9:00 a.m., he said in a firm voice, "Go right." Then I realized he was saying, "Go write." He sometimes commands me like I'm a kid. I find that incredibly endearing and cute. He tells me he thinks I am a kid. As if the tribulations of my life didn't leave a negative imprint. In fact, they didn't, and he's right. I'm weathered and beaten too. Who isn't? Tribulations left their imprint, but it is in terms of lessons learned and a mounting gratitude for having made it to the other side. Those trials served to categorize just about everything else that happens as trivial issues. I'm learning to simply not react to the small stuff. It's pretty much all small stuff.

What? You want to tell me something?

Letter to Mom

Tribulations, trials and trivial. Nice alliteration.

Everything is energy, Mom. Manage your triggers and your reactions, and watch the universe serve you up a feast.

I want to tell you what happened just after I crossed over. I was met by your Grandmother Emily, her friend Marjorie Greevy and Gabriel Rossy. They call themselves the G Team. Mom, it was great to see Marjorie. I didn't know Gabriel, but he is so cute! I recognized Grandma from your logo and that photo, but otherwise she looks a lot younger. She looks about 40 and wears her silver-grey hair in two long pigtails. Marjorie also looks a lot younger than I remember. Do you realize that we all choose our ages here? Gabriel chose to be about 28, and I chose to stay at 28. So I'm ageless, Mom. One difference is I've reclaimed my long, curly hair.

Gabriel and I were an item right from the start. Did you set that up?

I'll tell you about Gabriel later. The short answer is yes.

He has this way of stopping talking in mid-sentence and staring at me, like he wants to memorize me or something. It's like what you were doing after I died.

Mom, that was a bit kinky, no? Staring so long at that body? That's why I had to say that really gross, rude thing when you went to identify it at the funeral home. I wanted to make you laugh, and it worked. Please don't repeat it because it's gross—ignominious, actually. Another great word.

I know you were a bit freaked out by having to do that: identify the body of your daughter lying in a box, her lips sewn up. It took a lot of courage to go through that alone. I know that image haunts you.

It does. I couldn't believe that bit of protocol. Apparently, there was a body mix-up once, so now there has to be an ID before cremation. I really wish I'd had some strong arms to hold me that day.

It's strange how the detail of that little floral-printed smock thing they put you in stays with me. I remember thinking that it was a print better suited to an old lady. The thought that they plan only for old ladies went through my mind. I had a moment, a flash, that all of this was some strange mistake, and maybe you would open your eyes.

A plain, pine box. Your perfect dark curls. That nose. Some moments are colossally tough to accept, even though I know the universe makes no mistakes. Acceptance, acceptance. A hard-won truth that all is as it should be. That moment changed me.

"You had the blues, but you shook them loose."

You are irreverential. There's another one for you: 13 letters.

I wanted to make you smile—comic relief from emotional overload.

I think the funeral director thought it was a sob, but it was shock and laughter mixed together. I had to get out of there fast so that I wouldn't crack up for real. What a strange moment. I couldn't believe you said that. You have no shame!

Shame is useless, Mom. Like that empty shell in the box: of no use.

It mattered to me. It represented the physical you. Every precious hair on that head mattered. Every small touch of you. Every one of those long eyelashes. Those dark, large eyes. Each freckle. They mattered.

I know, I know.

You were a star at the funeral parlour. With all those people, you carried it off: the speech, the place, the tea and cupcakes, the casual and informal atmosphere. Thank you, Granny, for the forest of flowers that encircled the urn.

You stepped up. You knew I was beside you the whole time, the whole way, and that helped us both. And you spent five solid hours in those heels. Impressive! Thanks, Uncle Jay; you were kind and wonderful. Thanks, Auntie Lou. Thank you, thank you, thank you. I hugged each person. Every single one.

And then there was Isi. He didn't recognize you at first. The grey hair changed your look so completely. That explains why he didn't approach right away. Then he stayed all afternoon, chatting up the whole family. Coming close, hugging and terrorizing. "I should be here beside you," he said.

"You should," you said. The air between you was thick.

Mom, I always told you I thought you should go back to Isi. I thought you were crazy to have left him. I didn't understand that love is about the good and the bad times. After going through so many bad times, looking around for him and realizing he wasn't there, the good times started to mean less. They were still good, but they became kind of trivial, small. Those bad times when he was nowhere to be found became larger and larger, until there was no more space for anything else. I know how sad you were to wake up from cancer surgery alone. People can't give what they never receive.

Clo, I really loved that man. I wanted to grow old with him. It was simply not meant to be. We weren't able to figure out how to communicate, how to value each other and above all else, how to love. I kept leaving him and returning, attracted as a moth to a flame.

I awoke this morning, still clinging to a dream that I took a lit match and gently let it drop into a sewer grate. As it fell, the light began to extinguish until it hit the water at the bottom and went out with a very low, soft hiss. It's over. That flame is out. Fifteen years, and it's now over. Time to let go.

Fifteen years.

Remember the time you picked me up after I had been on the streets for two weeks? Mom, I still can't believe how I survived. I ate out of garbage bins. I—ate—out—of—garbage—bins. Do you get that?

Fuck.

The guys from the African store told me you'd been by looking for me. It took me a few hours to clear my head enough to call you. By that time, you were an hour and a half away. But I called you, and you came back. That was love, Mom. It was Friday afternoon. You'd just reached the country. And you came back for me.

Of course I came back for you.

I remember telling you to not move, to stay exactly where you were. I said I'd be right there. It was in about two hours, but I'd come for you. That was a stressful drive down, wondering if you would have bolted again or if you would be there. You were there, sitting at Tim Horton's. You were wearing dirty, ill-fitting clothes. You had two different shoes on; one was a rubber clog that was completely ripped at the toe. Your hair was a mess. You actually looked so beautiful and tanned despite the blisters on your lips. I chastised myself for having that superficial thought. You were tanned because you were living outside. You looked like a crazy, homeless person. You *were* a crazy, homeless person.

I took you up north. You had two baths, a haircut, a hot meal, and a 15-hour sleep in a lovely, comfortable bed. I threw away the clothes.

Isi didn't want me in the house. It's understandable when I look back. So you took me elsewhere, and that helped you leave him.

It did.

I was seriously messed up.

You were. Living with you was intolerable while you were coming down from your addiction to crack. I had no idea that you were living a withdrawal. I simply thought you were crazier than ever. Jerking movements of head, body, hands and arms. The rough flinging back of the neck. The screams and glares and outbursts of mean, filthy talk.

After two weeks of caring for you nonstop, I had to take a break, or else I'd break. I left you alone in the house and went for a walk. Something nudged me to check a local newspaper stand,

and by chance I found an ad for a residence only 15 minutes away that would take in people with mental health issues. I called.

Within a few days, you moved into Yves' house. He was a Godsend, literally a gift from the divine. You were safe, well cared for and subject to a certain structure of house rules that gave you limits. Your meals were prepared, and your money was well-managed.

Only then did I realize how I'd been living a stressed-out nightmare, sleeping with one eye open and constantly on edge. Even my eyeballs were on edge. I remember going to the optometrist. He couldn't give me a proper eye exam because my irises were constantly spasming.

"Stress," he said.

You have no idea, I thought. And yet I always managed to smile, to carry on, to run my business, to pay the bills. It was exhausting.

I'd had such good training as a young girl for this role of put up and shut up. Of being seen and not heard. Of caring so much what others thought of me. Of wanting to portray someone happy, satisfied, successful. What bullshit.

When you went to Yves', I finally slept soundly. What relief.

A few years before, I had visited Vilnius, Lithuania. The steps up to the Gate of Dawn, the holiest of shrines in Eastern

Europe, were deeply curved from all the pilgrims who had slowly ascended on their knees. I was staying a five-minute walk away. One morning, I ascended to the shrine, the only pilgrim at that early hour. I looked at the Black Madonna and asked, "Mary, I came all this way. What would you like to tell me?"

I heard these words loud and clear in my head: "No matter who, no matter what, always show mercy."

Those precious words helped me to not react to your insanity during those two weeks you came down off crack. They helped me when you barked orders at me. They helped me when you heaped verbal abuse on me. They helped when both you and your brother were ill, and I would work all day, go to one hospital psych ward and then head across town to another psych ward so I could visit you both. I learned the true power of that affirmation.

I also learned that the desire for control in an uncontrollable situation can make a person mean. I witnessed that in you throughout the day, in countless small ways. From the way you ordered me to refill your hot water bottle to your demand for tea, to your dark and mean looks that conveyed anger and victimhood.

"No matter who, no matter what, always show mercy."

Rinse, repeat.

Clo, you were like the *Challenger* space disaster of 1986. Seventy-three seconds into the flight, it exploded, killing seven astronauts. A meticulously, well-planned adventure that started with brilliant hope self-destructed shortly after takeoff. Freezing O-ring seals were the cause. The devil's always in the details. There had been warnings; they had been ignored. It was the same with you.

Grade nine, Mom.

Yup, grade nine. I remember how the transition happened almost overnight, once you decided you wanted to fit in, to be cool and popular. Up until that point, you had been the nerd who won most of the prizes at school. I remember specifically how you won every single prize except for music, when you graduated from elementary school. As the principal kept calling you up for history, mathematics, science and French, a sense of foreboding came over me. I knew you hadn't been invited to one grad party—not one—and you were so miserable.

You started high school innocently enough, but when the hormones kicked in and you got your period in grade nine, your breasts began to form, and your physical body began to dominate. Reason disappeared. The mental and the rational were left behind in the dust. You wanted popularity. You wanted friends. It started with marijuana, that not-so-innocent gateway drug.

I tried to keep you interested in swimming and lifeguarding, but soon you were telling me to fuck off. You were stomping out the door, swearing, not doing your homework and skipping classes. Your grades plummeted. The school vice principal, recollecting on how smart you were and how much you had helped the newcomers, tried to help you.

It was no small miracle that you made it through grades 10 and 11. Temporarily, you straightened out enough to finish two years of college and graduate with honours. When you were accepted as one of 60 students out of a field of 900 for the journalism program at university, I hoped your ship would sail correctly, but it was not to be. Just three weeks into the program, you walked out of a test, declared you were quitting school and went AWOL from your life.

It wasn't long before you were out of control.

The moment I cut my hair, I cut ties with my nerdy self. I had a short, sassy haircut and a new cocky attitude, and nothing could stop me. Nothing, not even you. I know you tried. I remember when you went to that five-week course on how to help steer your kids away from drugs. I remember when you met with the high school VP. He was such a cool guy. I even remember when you found the weed and called the police. You wanted them to bust me, to scare me a bit. They didn't even show up.

Mom, from here I can see everything you did to help. I can also see all the times you didn't quite make the grade as Mom of the Year. Get my drift? Everyone should know that everything is known.

I get your drift. I did the best I could with what I knew at the time, with the tools I had at the time. There were weekends I went up north with Isi when I should have stayed with you, taken you away from your delinquent friends or shipped you out of the city entirely. I could make myself crazy with regret.

But you won't. Right?

I won't. When it creeps up, I'll breathe and ask for peace in my heart. "Holy Spirit, show me the way to peace."

Chapter 3

Letter to Clo

I heard a saying today: "Marriage is a deeply strange thing to do to someone you love." How true! Talk about an almost foolproof way to mess up something great. Take two people and put them in close quarters. Then throw in money tension, job uncertainty, a crying and colicky baby, maybe a meddling in-law, his ex-girlfriend who is just a bit too cute and home repairs. The possibilities are endless.

Disney did us a major disservice. We all bought into the concept of romance and love everlasting with the endgame being the wedding. Remember when the wedding scene was the final scene in all those Hollywood movies?

Your dad was handsome and mysterious, and he worked as a DJ in a local bar. One night when I was underage, I tried to get in using my older sister's ID. He took one look at the card, smiled that beguiling smile and told me to come back after my birthday. I did.

We both loved Motown music. He spun the records; I danced the night away on the dance floor. That should be enough reason to marry, right? I knew nothing about what marriage entailed, nothing about real life after the parties are over. I was naïve and deliberately deaf to that wise voice inside me that kept saying, "Don't do it!"

I know so little about relationships, Mom. Mine were always messed-up power struggles.

They *are* power struggles. The struggle is whether the past will have the power to govern our present. They exist for us to learn and grow, not to live happily ever after.

It turns out that the individual you're lusting after (a necessary component to hook you in) is the prime pusher of your buttons. He chose you to complete his issues with his mother. You chose him to recreate the dynamic, to examine and hopefully resolve your issues with your father. And you thought it was about happily ever after. Ha! Your dad was a great teacher.

Take John: sweet, kind and loving—and traumatized by women. He's confused. Who isn't? Unlike some men, he is verbal, so he tells me he's still messed up about other women. He needs space.

Now the choice is mine. How do I handle this? Do I stay?

Do I bolt? I can choose not to react. Instead of packing my bags and stomping off, I can take a few breaths and be patient with myself, and with him. I choose to stay. I choose to be a witness to his words, not a defendant.

I stop, look up and ponder the magnificent sunrise. After a few breaths, I can handle his words without reacting. I'm helped by the beauty of this place; it opens my heart and smooths over the tough spots.

Yesterday, I missed you a lot and had a really good cry—big sobs. I need to minimize distractions and keep writing. It's the 80/20 rule: I decide my time must be 80 percent everything else, 20 percent John.

I'm not sure about this project, the theme, the layout, the content. I'm not sure about John. I am sure that you're fine and that you're with me. I am sure that I was guided to be here, so for now, that's enough.

My life experience feels like a collection of themes, Clo. I see them clear as day. How we're all walking wounded, living with loss and dealing with the anxiety of inevitable death. Grappling with mental health issues in children when all I wanted was to love you and help plan your wedding. Trying to be a conscious parent while I was trying to decipher my own life at the same time—and messing up on both. Forgiving others and myself, and making room for acceptance, allowance and non-reactivity. Seeing the truth that there is only life after life, and endeavouring to help shift the death paradigm to something less awful, less tragic.

Clo, help me do this.

I am.

After John claims he is mixed up and needs space, and he is escorting me out the door back towards my cottage, we see a dead bird on his patio. *This thing is dead,* I tell myself. *As dead as that bird.*

Then a call and a push of the reset button. "Could we go back?" he asks. "Could we date like people normally do when they're getting to know each other?"

"Sure," I say. "It's Tuesday. How about we go on a date Friday night? How about we stay away from each other till then?"

We agreed.

By Wednesday evening, he's sending me texts. "It's really stormy. Where are you? Drive carefully. I cleaned out your fireplace and filled up the kindling. Set up a fire so that when you get home, it's ready to be lit."

Then an invitation. "Would you like to come for breakfast Thursday morning?"

"Okay," I say, "but no surreptitious sneaking over in my PJs and crawling into your bed. Text me when you want me to come over."

He's dressed and ready and a bit aloof. A small hug, a kiss on the cheek. I just go with it. He makes toast, eggs and coffee. We sit on opposite couches, and mostly he talks about his work, his kids, his ex-wife, his difficulty letting go of his position in the realty business he founded and sweated over for 35 years.

I understand his internal struggle. Letting go of my business after living and breathing it for two decades meant a shift to seeing myself as more than my title as founder of Grandma Emily's Granola. GEG gave me identity; it gave me credibility. The ego loved that recognition. Yet the heart was saying, "Let go. Time to discover new paths, new challenges."

I listen and listen. He talks and talks. No hugging or kissing this morning; just two friends sitting and facing each other on two couches with two cups of coffee. I know, deep inside me, that this self-control is good for me. Getting my impulsive side under control is no small feat. It is the same energy, on the flip side, that gives me the courage to leap, the resilience to bounce back and the toughness to not pity myself for too long. Pick myself up, dust myself off, and start all over again. Impulsiveness and spontaneity—two sides of the same coin.

After breakfast, I have the strangest feeling that I passed some kind of test. I'm not sure what it was, but something lifted. I believe he's beginning to trust me.

"Do you still want to go on a date tomorrow night?" I ask.

"Yes," he says. He's reserved a table at one of his favourite spots. No lie, Clo, we get to the restaurant, and his ex-wife is sitting at our table with a friend. Mix-up of names and times. She thinks the table is hers. What to do but smile and offer a firm handshake?

Letter to Mom

Mom, you don't get it. When a person suffers a loss like you have, it's totally normal to want to connect with people afterwards. It's like the emotional body needs to get close to another emotional body. John is trying to figure out whether you want just hugs, or whether you really want him.

When did you get so wise?

Do you remember the best time you were with Isi? It was just after his mother died. Do you remember how you were so happy during this time? His heart had been opened by grief; he was more loving. You were so happy to receive and give affection to him. It didn't last long enough, though, and he fell back into being removed, aloof, distant and unloving. That made you so sad.

So that explains the need for a hug. John asked you yesterday what he can do for you. Tell him you need to be held. That is what you need.

Letter to Clo

I told him. Thanks. His hugs are amazing. He asked me what he could do to lose weight and feel better. He's opened the door, and now I can offer advice.

I suggest he cut his coffee to two cups a day. He suffered from gout in the past. I explain that he needs to balance the acid and alkaline levels in his body, drink more water and take apple cider vinegar (ACV) three times a day. He needs to make fruits and vegetables a bigger part of his diet, especially cherries because they're great for gout. He should forget about take-out. I also made him a batch of granola.

This is basic stuff, but to him it's news. And he listens. Now that he's taking the ACV, I'll introduce a squeezed lemon in water first thing every morning. It astonishes me that he doesn't know these fundamentals. It means changing the ritual of a coffee first thing. After just a few days, he's already sleeping better and feeling better. He stopped his gout meds too.

I don't know how to repair fibreglass, how to change a tire, how to replace a brake pad or a shock absorber, how to use a chainsaw, how to do plumbing or heating or ventilation or tiling. There are many things I have no clue about. But I do know about nutrition and well-being. Grandma knew. Mom knew. I grew up drinking fresh juice and watching my mother do a free-standing yoga headstand in the hallway. Eventually, I knew too. There's nothing quite so powerful as generational osmosis.

Just pulled the Star card in the Thoth tarot deck; it represents a complete breakdown of the old life, now in the process of creating something new and wonderful. What a perfect card. I trust that it is correct, coherent and good. This process is about what I want. It's about desire and dreams and manifesting them. I am at that place right now. I know that to simply have success in service is not enough. I want the relationship that makes everything magic. The sharing that gives meaning to every morning and night. The togetherness that manifests kindness, giving and loving. I want this deeply, more than anything else. This card tells me I am doing just that.

Clo, we are no longer in a mother-daughter relationship. It is now one kindred soul to another. I welcome this great collaboration. I love you deeply, and I am here to serve.

Letter to Mom

Hi, Mom. I have a new dilemma: what to call you? Mom seems too subordinate. Andrea seems too egalitarian. How about "Yo, Kid"? Just kidding!

Mom, he's not going to change; he is who he is. If you can't accept him as he is, then don't accept him and leave now. Otherwise, you'll become frustrated. Know that our habits are so difficult to change. Can you stay independent? Can you stay objective?

How do you really feel about him? You think you love him. That's a big thing. He's got lots of baggage, lots of dents and bumps. So do you. A woman who's suffered the trauma of losing a child, of having a son who's schizophrenic. A woman who is dedicated to bringing about spiritual awareness in others, who's not working, who is a writer, who is so different from him. A woman who has no home and so is something of a flight risk. A woman who never watches TV.

In your mid-50s, with much life experience and wisdom, you also have a lot to bring to the table. So don't undersell yourself.

You have work to do—a book to finish and a mission to pursue. John can provide comfort; you asked for this. You can provide calm; he asked for that. You both can offer each other good company.

Letter to Clo

Thanks for those words. Un jour à la fois.

I'm excited that we're going to work together in order to bring Matthew to a place of greater openness to healing. Matthew always resented sharing me with you and your brother Daniel. Now he doesn't have to. When we're together, my attention is focused solely on him. I leave my cell phone in the car. Three hours a week isn't much, but it's a major improvement over the past. Am I expecting too much?

You may have not known this, but I used to sleep with pepper spray by my bedside, to protect myself. Matthew was highly volatile. Initially he was diagnosed as bipolar, but I never saw any depressed mood. I witnessed only his mania, his pacing, lots of yelling, threats with knives and destructiveness in the house. The correct diagnosis came eventually. Schizophrenia.

I knew I should have called the police but couldn't bring myself to turn in my own son, my firstborn. My role was to protect, guide and support him. On the other hand, he terrorized me. I lived in fear.

One particular day stands out in my memory. We were in the kitchen, and Matt picked up a large knife. "If I were you," he said, waving the knife in the air, "I think I'd kill myself because your life is so pathetic."

How to describe what pure terror feels like? It was as if my blood stopped pumping. I had no breath. Forget the knife—just the fear was enough to do me in. He lost me that day. Now that I think of it, he did kill something inside me. I knew it wasn't Matt speaking; I knew it was an illness. It simply became too real that day: the unpredictability, the risk, the potential for tragedy. It was my own child talking like this. Something unravelled inside me.

I wanted to get out of my life. Slowly I started giving all my things away, starting with my jewellery. Then it was clothes, furniture and dishes, until finally I put my beloved home up for sale. That hurt, but I knew I couldn't live with him anymore.

Another letting go. Another loss.

Clo, I worked so hard to pay for that house, finance my business and pay for everything for the three of you. I loved every piece of furniture, every plant, every corner, every angle, the way the sun came in at all different times of the day. It was my refuge—until it no longer was. It became a prison, and your brother was my jailor.

I remember you redoing my room to help me restart my life. You repainted all my furniture.

Painting was like meditation. Remember when we were in that leaky rental house for five years? I must have painted every room. I remember putting four, five coats on the dining room walls before I had the deep raspberry colour I wanted. A few days after finishing the room, we had a major rain storm overnight. In the morning, the outside dining room wall was six months pregnant! A huge ball of water had gathered under the windowsill, trapped inside all those coats of paint. I laughed so hard.

Somehow, some small sliver of self-control kept him from hurting me. Another time, he jumped out of the car when we were on the freeway and stuck in traffic. We were going slowly enough for him to jump out. But then what to do? I had to pull over and walk back to him, all the while with cars going by. I was trying to talk him into getting back in the car.

Did he?

No. He ran off. I had no idea whether he would run into traffic and get hit, or whether he would come home. The stress was over the top. And I told no one. I was too embarrassed by the stigma, too freaked out by his actions, too ashamed. I felt guilty and responsible.

Meanwhile, he had done mind-destroying drugs, and his brain's wiring had been affected. I didn't know, and I didn't know what he was capable of doing. Living with that kind of uncertainty made life a living hell.

And then you had me heading off the rails.

Yup. And I was trying to run a business.

I lived this stressful home life, barely sleeping at night. During the day, I'd be the entrepreneur. I couldn't quite figure out whether I was a complete phony or had the resilience of a prize fighter. Maybe I was both. Only your brother Daniel knew what I was living. He would take off travelling for months at a time; those escapes kept him sane. That was his big worry: "If this happened to my siblings, will it happen to me too?" I was worried about that.

One day I went to the local police station to show Matt's photo. I explained that they might find him roaming the streets, and that I felt he could be violent. They already knew him! He had gone there just days prior, asking them to put a bullet in his brain to take him out of his misery. I cried when the officer on duty told me that. Can you imagine being so desperate to want someone to shoot you?

That's when the officer explained that this type of illness first terrorizes the victim himself. That's why they sometimes attack police officers, so that they can be shot and put out of their misery. The officer called it assisted suicide. He went on to recount how he had spent a lifetime dealing with his adult brother's mental illness before his brother finally took his own life. Is there one family that is not touched by mental illness?

Oh, the irony. On the walls of the police station were plaques of drawings done by school kids who had won a competition to describe the importance of the community police station. Matthew's drawing had won first prize. He had been 7 years old.

I had to let go of the concept of saving Matthew. At 17, he was earning a thousand dollars a day cold-calling and selling spa coupons on the street. It was a tough job, and he was good at it. Too good. That was the beginning of the end. Some of that money went to hard drugs. The hard drugs went to the brain. End of story.

I finally took steps to have him picked up by the police and brought to the hospital. I had to prove he was a danger to either himself or someone else. He was both. Two police officers, two ambulance workers and I cornered him. They actually had to handcuff him. I was devastated and said, "How much can I take, Lord?"

Those moments almost seem like they happened in slow motion, in an effort to have every detail remain vivid in my memory. Matt screaming at the police, the aggression of the police officers, the straightforward and no-nonsense first responders. I wasn't prepared for Matt's anger and hate being directed at me for having tricked him into being cornered.

The first few times I went to see him in the hospital, he spat at me, angry that I had put him there. Even though it took almost an hour to drive to the hospital in rush-hour traffic, sometimes I stayed only minutes. I couldn't allow him to abuse me without a consequence. Where did I find the strength to calmly say, "Matt, I'll see you soon. Maybe next time you'll feel less angry"?

He spent six months in intensive care. It was a strange place, with not one machine. No beeps or flashing red lights. The nurses wore jeans and didn't have stethoscopes around their necks. It was care for the brain, and there wasn't much to be done besides medicate and wait. I went to see him almost every day after work.

Then you got sick, Clo. I could no longer function as an entrepreneur, a coach and a mentor to other young people. I had to take some distance to try to keep my sanity through all that heartache.

It felt like picking at skin till it started bleeding, except that it wouldn't stop. I felt raw, uncovered, exposed.

Excoriated.

Precisely. Thank you.

Sunday night family dinners with my siblings felt like torture. Nieces and nephews were smiling and laughing and getting on with their lives. Two of my children were conspicuously absent. How to not let that tear my heart out? How to act normal, to find my bearings when true north was no longer true?

I had to let go of the concept of family as it used to be. I had to let go of the desire to heal you, to save you. I let go of the desire to hug you, to have a decent conversation. I also let go of the hope that all would be different for you and for Matthew.

I looked for tools. Yoga, breathing, exercise, meditation, affirmations, Reiki—it all helped to maintain some sense of normalcy. But eventually, I had to drop all the tools and live many dark nights of the soul. Knowing I am not alone, knowing I'm loved and knowing that all is as it should be in the end were the three great knowings that pulled me through.

And so all is well. We continue to muddle through at this end, trying to make sense of the signs, trying to listen and be inspired and do the right thing. We're trying to make the right choices and not mess up our lives too much. We're trying to read the red flags, to decipher a flag from a mere puff of red smoke. How to know when it's wrong? How to know when it's over, or when something great is just beginning? There is so much input happening from every corner of the room, so many emails to answer, so much online news to read and comments to give, so much digital deluge. How to know what matters and what doesn't? So many questions.

And still I have no answers. I do have words. They keep spilling out in a vain attempt to make sense of this grief, this joy, this well-being that happens when I'm out in nature. I have this sense that I no longer want to live in the city. I want to trudge around in my red Billy boots. I want to plant, to plunge my hands in the soil, to live where the sky fills with the lights of millions of worlds at night. I want to hear birds, to be near water. I want to talk to you and hear you reply. I want to feed the ducks and to grow edible flowers.

I want to bake, to take a handful of ingredients and make something wonderful. Add this, add that, bake and voila! A delicious masterpiece to eat. I want to care for someone. I want to be joined to others, not alone. Sometimes I do want to flee. Old habits die hard.

I want to connect to you. I'm playing "Staralfur" by Sigur Ros right now. My heart cries. This is purposeful grieving. I deliberately brought it on myself, as if I needed to purge some sadness.

I wonder if I'm attracted to John simply because loss prompts the desire for emotional connection to others. Is he just here to fill that need? Should I be with someone who takes better care of himself? He smokes! That was my one deal breaker. I had my thyroid gland removed due to cancer. Smoking is gross—I should know. I preferred smoking to eating from the age of 16 to 26. Then I quit.

I meet John and toss that deal breaker out the window. What is it that attracts me to him? Am I still addicted to saving other people? To wanting to change or rescue them so that they'll love me enough and never reject me? Haven't I let that go yet?

Does any of it matter? A connection with another human being happens on the nonverbal level much more deeply than because we like to eat from the same food groups. Everything is energy. Attraction has no true explanation in the rational mind. Am I attracted? Intensely. Perhaps that's enough for now. Ultimate loving of other human beings is all about accepting them as they are. You taught me that. I watched you smoke, flounder, crash and burn. There was nothing to say, no saving to do. You were on your path, and all I could was watch and accept. That is unconditional loving. Is my loving of John conditional because I want to assist him to eat better, to feel better, to care better for himself?

As of this moment, I will give him no more advice unless he asks.

I just reread my words above, and one phrase jumps out at me: purposeful grieving. Directed, not random or hysterical. Sadness experienced the way my heart wants to feel it. Nothing to add or subtract. Nothing to assuage or calm or talk away. No affirmations to make, or deliberate thinking to recite in rote. Just grief washing over me. Allowing it doesn't cause me to break into a million pieces. Who knew this pain wouldn't kill me?

Knowing you're close is triggered by small things like cigarette smoke. At random moments, I smell that acrid, distinctive smell. There is no mistaking it. But no one around is smoking. It could only be you.

Why come at this moment?

Just to let you know I'm near. To encourage you to write.

I sense I should be writing, but I'm not sure what to write about. So I write what I know.

You know about loss. You know about facing death. You know that life is magic. You know how to find the magic in the tragic. Ma, you know lots of things. You know how to open your heart.

I used to think, *Everyone knows what I know. They all realize that death is not the end but simply the end of the physical body. There's nothing special about what I know.* But then I witnessed the things people said and felt at funeral parlours. So many people were so freaked out by death.

I'm so glad you were happy with the way the funeral parlour went. It was short, sweet and wonderful. We had the entire place, and the room downstairs was well set up for tea and cupcakes. We had a room for viewing the photos. Flowers were well-distributed, and the enormous bouquet that surrounded your urn was lovely. I was happy to have spoken so well. I didn't falter or fade, didn't crumble into boatloads of tears. I simply held it strong, held it together so that I could tell a story, make people laugh, take the high road and thank everyone.

That was a great story. Totally true and funny. Thanks for that.

Presenting a less morose, less terrible aspect of death will irritate some, rub up acceptingly with others and may brand me crazy. No amount of criticism can silence me any longer. It doesn't matter anymore because I know what I know, and all I want to do is offer it out. I don't want to convince, convert or persuade anyone of anything. So here goes.

I'm with you.

When the critics get too loud, I'll keep repeating that famous phrase attributed to Eleanor Roosevelt: "What you think of me is none of my business."

Love that one.

Letter to Mom

Mom—a tough habit to break this "Mom" thing, because Mom is Mom, for all of us. So for now, I'm going to stick to that.

The funeral parlour was perfect. It was me: casual and warm. I was amazed so many people came. And all those cards, calls and emails. Boy, death makes people take notice of life, no?

Mom, I'm in the wish-fulfilment business. It's time to have your wishes fulfilled. How was last night?

Clo, it was my wishes fulfilled. We actually made it through dinner in a very civilized fashion before things got wonderfully, deliciously uncivilized.

News flash: What we tell ourselves while we're tuning in and turning on is key. If we're thinking about an ex, a movie star, how to make a soufflé or whatever, others will sense it on an energetic level. If we tell ourselves that our partners are the sexiest, the most desirable ever, and that we want to love them madly and totally, they'll feel that too.

My demure and graceful mother of three, entrepreneur, writer, speaker, actor, volunteer, philanthropist—and sex therapist! Ha!

I'm just saying what I know to be true. At the risk of stating the obvious, great sex is all in the head. Great sex makes a difference, and we can make it great by the thoughts we think.

Great sex is in the head.

Great sex makes a difference.

We can make it great by the thoughts we think.

Clo, would that qualify as a haiku?

Not like the ones I wrote. Why didn't we have this conversation when I was alive?

It's easier to talk to you about it now; now that the barriers are down. We can talk about everything, like a couple trying to repair a marriage after an affair has been acknowledged. The old way has been torn down, disassembled. It's sitting in a disintegrated heap on the living room floor. It's rebuilding time, and the time is now or never. Therefore all subjects are fair game. Nothing is taboo any longer. The conversation gets real, authentic and valuable. The old relationship is dead. Same thing is happening here.

So no more bullshit. No more being stuck with old ways of thinking that you can't say this or can't do that.

Exactly.

I do wish we'd had this kind of openness while we both sat at the kitchen table.

Me too.

On another subject, I'm trying to write a play.

A what?

A play. I had this discussion with Callie, my friend who's a theatre director. She's guiding me. I've finally realized that it's okay to ask others for help. She asked me pointed, real questions about my play, the message I want to convey, what the central character is living and how my audience can relate to him. She explained that the audience has to feel something for this main character: empathy, sympathy, affection, hatred, something.

Mom, what's the play about?

It's about life and death, and how a man spends the last 30 days of his life. However, he doesn't know he has as long as 30 days to live. Every day, he awakes thinking it's his last day. He receives visitors from history who discuss issues big and small with him. By day eight, he stops caring if it's his last day and decides to enjoy living that day and the people with whom he interacts.

Seems like a strange premise for a story.

It may seem strange, but that's what the father of modern philosophy, Socrates, lived at the end of his life.

No kidding!

No kidding.

Wasn't he poisoned?

Poisoning was the way his death sentence was carried out. He was condemned to die, but Greek law required that the heads of state be present. They were not present and were delayed by poor weather from returning to Athens. Their boats couldn't travel. So Socrates languished in his jail cell for 30 days.

Mia the cat, doing her job

I read the last speech he gave before drinking the hemlock, and I was inspired. I thought about what those 30 days were like and decided to write a play about it. I started it while you and I were living your last summer.

There was a lot of time to write, especially by the end of the summer, when you began to sleep a lot. Instead of wanting to drive all the time, you curled up on the sofa with your little Mia curled up on top of you, and you slept. So, I wrote.

Can I read it? I need your permission.

Sure. It's not very good. Actually, according to Callie, it needs a lot of work. Right now it's just a discussion about philosophy. The characters don't have dimension. We feel no empathy for the main character of Socrates. There is no reason for the audience to love him, hate him or otherwise. There isn't enough to capture our hearts and keep us in our seats. And those are the good parts.

Sounds pretty bad.

I thought it was pretty good, but what do I know?

Can I try my hand with it?

Sure, Clo. Be my guest.

That's it, Mom!

What's it, Clo?

That's the title: "Be My Guest." I'm going to call the play "Be My Guest," and it's going to be about Socrates' last 30 days and the guests that come to see him. But it's going to be about how a man who's condemned to die spends what time he has left.

Clo, kinda sounds like your life. Who better than you to know what it feels like to have so little time left? Hmm, I like that. I think on some level, we can all relate to loss. We all live loss. Socrates, in the short space of time he has left, is alive long enough to face his losses square in the face. Loss of contact with his family. Loss of his friends, his work, his beloved city. Loss of his physical body. Some losses will bother him more than others. That should be fascinating. We've had a bit of experience, eh, Clo?

Yes, Mom, we have.

That was some discussion, no? Sex and Socrates in the same evening. Love you. Good night.

Bonne nuit, Maman.

Chapter 4

I'm getting mixed up. I don't know whether this is a letter to Clo or a letter to Mom. Our conversations are so fluid now. I'm writing to you; you pop in with a comment, and I record it. Letters have become one conversation. I can't keep track of who's writing to whom anymore, so let's just call this a conversation. Okay?

Okay.

Clo, here's the article I sent in to the newspaper as a "Lives Lived" contribution. Not sure it will be printed, but writing it was cathartic. It has a different tone to our conversation because it isn't a conversation. I tried to write it like an obituary with a more personal touch—one step closer to a subjective, emotional piece but still objectively informative. I hope you like it.

Chloe—A Life Lived

When you were little, you loved to wear dresses. Even under your ski suit, you'd wear that dark blue velvet dress. A girly girl with a warrior's heart.

Sometimes I dressed us in jeans and gingham blouses, our hair done up the same. Off we went to the circus, to stroll Old Montreal like tourists, to eat ice cream or to skate in the park.

When you were well, we skied, cycled, travelled, hiked, snowshoed, kayaked and went swimming together. We cooked, danced and played tranka.

Mostly you swam, moving that graceful body of yours through the water, at ease. I loved to watch you swim.

When you were well, we took a road trip, breaking into that campground after the doors closed, giggling and fumbling and finally dozing off in our half-mounted tent. And then, as mothers do, I accommodated your wish to travel solo, by flying home and leaving you the car to continue on your way. You made it back—banged up and scratched, but intact.

When you were well, you used words like circumspect and ignominious.

"Igno what?" I had to look it up. It means rude, shameful.

You developed colon cancer, had surgery and went through chemo. When the cancer got worse, we took to the countryside—you, your brother Daniel and I. We awoke every morning so grateful for that precious time together. Mia the kitten knew her role, spending hours lying across your belly and bringing comfort.

Just after Christmas, you went into palliative care. Just 28 years old. Activities dropped away until only breathing was left. Breathing and massage. Ever since you were little, I had given you massages under the guise of pedicures and manicures. I added a new spa treatment: facials. A facial was the perfect excuse to touch your face, deliberately committing every bone and curve to memory.

On the last afternoon of your life, after finishing a foot massage, I had a dilemma. To wash or to not wash the oil off my hands? Doing so would mean washing off the touch of your skin. I had a feeling it would be the last massage I would give you. It was.

As I sat with you long after the breath had ceased, I focused intently on the freckles of your left forearm, their pattern creating a new constellation of stars fused in my heart. Your father cut me a small lock of your hair.

If You Love Me, Weep No More

If you love me, weep no more.

Death is nothing.

I have only crossed over to the other side.

I am still me. You are still you.

What we were for each other we will always be.

Call me by the name you have always called me.

Speak to me as you have always spoken.

Do not use a different manner.

Do not fall solemn or sad.

Continue to laugh at what we used to laugh at together.

Pray, smile, think of me

That my name is spoken at home like it always was:

Simply, with no trace of incertitude.

Life symbolizes what it has always symbolized.

It is always what it has been, the thread is not broken.

Why would I be far from your thoughts

Simply because I have disappeared from your sight?

I am not far away, just on the other side of the road.

You see, everything is alright.

You will find my heart, you will find pure tenderness within it.

Wipe away your tears and weep no more if you love me.

—Saint Augustine

I believe him. I know you're in the next room and are well, happy and reunited with your whole self. If ever there was a reason to write a sad, grieving piece, this is it. But I cannot. I can only write what is in my heart, and my heart says, "Soar, my lovely one. You are whole. I love you. Everything is all right."

I love it, Mom. I remember when we did that stuff together. You're right: speak to me as you have always spoken. The conversation never actually ends. Most people know this. They keep talking to the ones they've loved who've passed. They hear the answers too, but they don't tell anyone because they're afraid of being branded crazy.

We both know it's only the physical that's ended, not the life.

It was weird that you took a picture of me on the last afternoon of my life, sent it to your brother Al and told him, "You won't see Chloe alive anymore," like you knew that was it.

I simply felt the nudge to take those shots. They're precious to me now.

Can you tell me more about Callie's comments? I'm getting into the idea of writing about the end of a life and what matters. What did she say?

Let me check my notes. They're a bit of a mish-mash, Clo. I wonder if all writers have scribbles on paper towels, airline napkins, the backs of menus, playbills and museum maps? You name it; I've written on it. Here goes: She said that even when you do a historical play, what makes it relevant is whether it's relevant now. Is what they're talking about in our modern discourse? The characters need to exhibit qualities that will engage the audience; this keeps them interesting.

She asked me, "What are you trying to say?" In a nutshell, it's about a man's last 30 days, the people he meets with and the conversations he has. We need a story, not a philosophical debate. Right now, it's only philosophy. Why are they even visiting him?

We don't want to be constrained by the audience having to know the figures who visit him.

My first draft included a man called Leo Baeck. I had read about him. He was a German Jew who worked to bridge understanding between the two peoples. His last act of defiance when the Nazis arrested him was to pay his electricity bill. This was lauded and applauded as a dignified act of citizenry when all around him, people were acting as barbarians.

But Callie said, "No one knows Leo. So, tell the electricity bill story and bring him to life. Forget the big, philosophical discussion about dying for your beliefs."

"The audience has to get to know the characters. Why are they even visiting Socrates? Is he conjuring them up? Are we following his psyche as he gets closer to death? What becomes urgent? What does he want by making that contact, and how is he changed by that contact? We need to care about the people we're following. We want our hero to get what he wants, so there needs to be something more personal at stake in those interactions."

Amazing feedback, no? Callie is a real pro. Socrates had no idea he would languish 30 days in his cell; every day could have been his last day.

What better person to take up this challenge than you, Clo? You know what it is to live with the awareness of a finite number of heartbeats ahead. We all live that way, but we're not all so acutely aware of that, are we? Isn't it incredible that 100 percent of us are going to die, yet we don't even want to talk about it?

We're talking.

Yup, we're talking, my lovely one. Having a little trouble breathing …

That's grief, Mom.

I need to be patient with myself. It feels like a piece of cement the size of a grapefruit is sitting in the middle of my chest. Who knew grief had something in common with grapefruits?

Breathe in, breathe out. Do you notice you keep staring at the lamp on your night table?

Yeah. What's that all about?

I'm trying to give you a metaphor for handling life.

Okay. I'm listening …

The night table beside your bed sits flush on the wall.

Yup.

It's not a large table, but you like to put lots of stuff on it. A couple of books, a lamp, your hand cream, a box of Kleenex, maybe a crystal or a few stones, your alarm clock, a pen, some lined paper to record a dream. All that on a small surface that's two feet by one foot.

Seems a bit crowded. But I need everything that's there. I need my stuff.

Okay. Think of that surface as your life. Now look at the lamp. What do you see?

The lamp? It reminds me of the shape of a woman. The lamp shade is the large hat on her head.

Excellent.

So? For the last three days, you've been directing my gaze to that lamp.

Even though the base of the lamp is small, the diameter of the shade's lower brim is large. Because of that wide brim, the lamp has to sit in the middle of the night table, cutting up the much-needed space.

Mama mia …

Seriously, look! It's taking up way too much space. The lamp should be flush with the wall to give you maximum space, but it can't because the brim's too large. It's not enough to have a small base of the lamp. You have to have a narrow lamp shade too.

Think of the shade as the head, the mind.

I'm too much in my head? The rational is crowding the process? It's taking up too much space?

Exactly. That shade will now be a constant reminder to you to get out of your head more often.

I'm not sure if you're nuts or brilliant.

Les deux?

You're right. Now when I look at it, I'll tell myself, "Self, get out of your head." Thank you. That took three days to decipher.

Better three days than three hours. Real learning takes time. Now it'll stick.

So, tell me briefly what you wrote about Socrates.

Phew. Okay, the action takes place in his cell. There's a jailor who represents the common man of his time. He's my version of the comic relief, only he's not actually comedic. He's the thread that ties the scenes together.

People keep coming to visit Socrates. I had Leo Baeck, John Lennon, Socrates's wife, Pythia (the oracle of Delphi), a local fisherman and Plato, Socrates's star pupil.

The scenes are kind of tied together by the physical act of Socrates constantly building an omphalos in his cell.

What's an omphalos?

Strange word, no? Socrates tells the legend of the omphalos. The god Apollo, son of Zeus, wanted to determine the centre of the world so that he could erect a temple there. He released two golden eagles to fly in opposite directions around the globe. The spot they met at was Delphi, Greece, so Apollo threw down a giant stone—the omphalos—and declared that spot the centre of the earth. It's about three feet high, has curved sides and a flat bottom and comes to a point at the top, like the tip of a bullet. It actually looks kinda phallic.

I went to Delphi. I loved those ruins of the Temple of Apollo, scattered all over Mount Parnassus. Because there is no city built up around them, you can feel how the people lived, and how the ruins once created a most majestic spot. I spent three days there. For me, three days in one spot is a lot.

The August heat was almost heart-stopping, but I spent hours walking amongst the ruins and imagining what Socrates must have experienced when he went there. He made many pilgrimages to visit the Oracle of Delphi from Athens over the course of his life.

The omphalos is there, on the ground. The idea of Socrates creating an omphalos is that the new centre of his universe is now his cell.

At the very beginning of the play, Socrates asks the jailor for a spoon. The jailor mocks alarm, asking if Socrates is planning on digging his way out. The jail cell is actually a cave, deep in a mountain's side, so the chances of that happening are nil. Socrates explains he's going to dig himself in, and the jailor hands him two spoons.

Subsequently, in different scenes, different people help add earth to the mound.

That's cool.

The fact that he has two spoons means that a guest can sit with him and help him build his mound of earth. It's kind of like an act of kinship, as well as some action in a play that otherwise is just dialogue.

Okay, I'll try my hand at this. How about if I write one scene, and you'll tell me how you like it? You can send it to Callie, if you like.

Good idea.

I've been thinking a lot about how we discuss death, how we prepare or don't prepare and what our culture offers as assistance. Death anxiety is real, and it prevents authentic conversations from taking place.

Like this one.

What's the story with Gabriel Rossy? How come he met me? Did you know him?

I met Gabriel after he died. Gabriel crossed over in August 2006. He was 27 years old. He had been driving in a heavy rain storm when an enormous tree, old and rotten, fell on his car. He was killed instantly.

I learned of his death but didn't contact his family at that time. Two weeks later, while brushing my teeth one morning, I kept hearing this phrase in my head: "Tell them I'm fat and happy. Tell them I'm fat and happy."

I knew this wasn't coming from me because it made no sense, yet it wouldn't stop. I finally stopped what I was doing and asked who this was. And Gabriel answered.

He spoke clearly and calmly and wanted to dictate a letter to his mother. I sat down and took dictation. Then I had the formidable task of calling his mother, Sharon. What to say? Her grief was fresh, and I didn't want to upset her any more than she already was over the tragic death of her eldest child.

Ignoring him was not an option; he was relentless. Gabriel absolutely wanted them to know he was okay and that he was actually happy. He explained to me that he had always found his body too skinny and had often remarked that he would have been happier if he had been a bit heavier. Then he showed me a scene, kind of like a movie, of him mowing the word "fat" into the lawn as he cut the grass.

I finally called Sharon, went to see her, delivered the letter and offered other evidence that he was indeed alive and well. I believe it brought her great comfort. She never really reacted to the lawn mower scene he had shown me, but I felt responsible to give what I got. Nothing more, nothing less.

On many occasions, Gabriel would visit and ask if he could chat, cycle or walk with me. One day he asked me to contact his younger brother, Justin. I hesitated because almost five years had passed since his death.

I finally called Justin after much insistence from Gabriel. I went over the information he had previously given me, and when I told Justin the story of his older brother cutting the word "fat" into the tall grass, Justin dropped the phone. That had indeed happened, but only Justin and Gabriel were there that day; his mother didn't know about it. Finally, Justin was given the stronger confirmation he had sought: that his brother was alive and well.

Gabriel and I keep in touch, and when he has something to tell his mom, like wanting to congratulate her on her academic achievements, I call Sharon up and relay the information.

Then one day, he asked me if he could do anything for me as a thank-you for listening and for trusting that I was not making this all up. You were ill by then, so I asked him to please look out for you, to be there to greet you and to welcome you. Also, I thought you'd love to be greeted by a handsome young man about your age.

And the rest is history.

That's a great story. Still being a meddling mom, trying to fix me up with a nice guy. I like that.

Me too. I did receive communication from another son who wanted to reach his mother, but I hardly knew her, so I felt I couldn't just call her up. I felt his desire to connect but didn't know how to reach out to her, so I didn't. Then I asked them to stop.

Look for the dots to connect, Mom. They will.

I hope so. Why have this gift if I don't use it to help grieving parents?

Chapter 5

Hi, Clo. I wanted to tell you what happened today. I went to visit the hospital staff that had cared for you. They were a bit surprised to see me because you've already been gone two months.

I took loaf cakes. I can't get over how hospital staff eat all day long, so I thought food would be appreciated. I feel almost silly telling you this because you know I went to see them. I know you know the conversations I had and the people I hugged on your behalf. They really cared about you, and it makes a difference that they know no matter how much time passes, that they are not forgotten.

Did you see the face of that young trainee in palliative care? The face of an angel. So many things about yesterday were cool. Please remember to visit them in another month or so.

I will.

My friend Sue is trying to teach me that I shouldn't settle for a man if being with him still makes me the smartest person in the room. But smart about what? I can be smart intellectually but really immature in other ways. No one person has it all, and we can all learn from each other. Naïve?

Yes and no.

Perfect answer.

Seriously, it changes with your age. You want and accept different things. Meet a boy at 16 or a man at 60, and what you're willing to accept is different.

I don't want to live with someone full-time. I don't want to do their laundry. I don't want to cook all their meals and clean up after them. I want to be cherished, treasured, loved, appreciated and never taken for granted.

Bravo.

It strikes me that here we are, having this amazing conversation across the great divide, and what are we talking about? Boys. It never changes, does it? There's lots of other stuff we could talk about too, like where are you, what you are doing, how you are living, what is living all about when you don't have a body? Help me out here.

We take on bodies, but the difference is that we know this is a dream moment. You actually think that what you're living is real when you're alive in a body. It's a dream. "Life is but a dream," remember?

Gabe and I are in a "relationship." We know we're doing this so that we can complete something unfinished in our last incarnations, the ones just finished. I really wanted it. It's kind of like what you and John are doing. You're kinda beginning to realize how much is play, make-believe. It all is. So live the moment with him and complete whatever you have to complete.

I totally heard you that night, by the way, when you told me to go, to let go. You had really shown me the way, Mom. You had let go of so much stuff, and I didn't even need to look for courage. I simply followed your lead.

Thanks, Clo. Tell me more.

Letting go is the way we move forward. We can't move forward if the handbrake's on. Daniel has to let go of the fantasy about his schooling. A sailor, after plying the seas for a year, lets go of the romantic fantasy of life on the sea; he now longs for land, for sameness, for company. You let go of the old expectations for all your children: that we would go to university, achieve our potential, be brilliant, accomplished. Let go, let go, let go. After consciously doing all that, death is a lot easier to accept.

What about sudden death?

There is no sudden death. All death is pre-planned; we simply may not be aware of it. Live like you can say goodbye. Live like you've already said the eulogy. Atone. Think about it, Mom. Atone. Find a tone that resonates and sing it out loud. Everyone should sing in whatever capacity, in whatever key. Your sound is you; let it rise up. In so doing, up goes the spirit.

Here are a few things you may want to know.

Once you cross over, you can assume any age you like. You can take on the physical characteristics of the human incarnation you just left, or any other one you've lived. The funny thing is you seem to look pretty similar physically from one life to the next, whether you choose to incarnate as male or female.

So much of the sexuality sequencing and mess-up is all about crossover from one life to the next. A person may identify very strongly with a past life as a female, be born a male, and then have this inner struggle to express that femininity with which he so strongly identified. This is getting even more pronounced as people begin to recall past lives more. Individuals with this more present yin-yang balancing are brave individuals who agree to come forth and provide a shifting perspective to traditional mores and beliefs about gender and sexuality.

You can choose any name too.

We are totally alive. Totally. Please stop getting so hysterical about our passing. Oh, and by the way, I've coined a new phrase to describe dying. I call it pushing the reset button. That's what it is—a reset. Very 21st century, no?

We keep creating, we keep growing and we keep evolving. We are not slumbering in some kind of suspended state, unless we really believe we will do that. In that case, our beliefs shape the experience we initially have once we die. When we're ready, we come out of that dream bit by bit, realize we're dead and begin living again. Sound simple?

Keep talking to us, keep talking about us and keep us alive. Here's a concept you may not have heard before: Take the picture of a saint—let's say Jesus. The more you gaze lovingly on his picture, pray to him and speak to him, the more you increase the power of that picture no matter where it exists on the planet. Is that a concept or what? That representation actually takes on more value as more people adore it. Such is the power of collective thought. It can also work in reverse, creating havoc and suffering if enough people focus on destructive thoughts. Don't underestimate your thoughts; they create real stuff. They create the collective consciousness that drives events.

There is no hell. Hell exists on earth, right now, right around the next corner. Just take a look at the evening news.

When you pray, you create a beam of light that shoots out into the universe. This is how we find you and communicate with you. It is a beautiful thing to see.

Everything we think, say and do as human beings is known. There are virtually no secrets. Remember that. When you review your life, it'll all be right there in front of you. And you will review, the better to process, plan, and regroup before the next adventure.

Our pets will greet us if that's what we believe will happen. In fact, whatever we believe is what happens. That's why it's essential to examine those beliefs before pressing that reset button.

Make it a grand exit, not a painful one. Believe it or not, you control that. You write the program, select the scenario and press the button when you're ready.

We are shifting towards death as a celebratory event. It won't be that way for everyone, but for more and more, it will be that way. Mark these words. Saint Augustine is rolling his eyes. "It's about time!" he says. It's only been 1,600 years since he wrote that the dead are just in the next room. Religious doctrines designed to instil fear and obedience have done much harm, creating a whole pack of untruths about death that disempower and frighten us. This is changing—finally.

We hear you. We hear you when we're in a coma. We hear you after we've passed. We hear you even if you think we don't. We do.

If a person dies a raging alcoholic, she still has to overcome that addiction on the other side. There is no escaping ourselves. There is no way of hiding our thoughts like we do as human beings. The freedom of no physical body, once you realize it, is the most amazing incredible feeling.

If you were loud and boisterous, you're still going to be loud and boisterous. If you were shy, you're still going to be shy. Your personality remains intact through millennia, only changing when you want to change it. It isn't changed by death. It's changed by realizing, "I'm going to stop, right now, judging and criticizing others. I'm going to stop gossiping. I'm going to focus on myself and let others focus on themselves." And it is done.

Every single person who crosses over is enveloped in a love that nurtures and comforts them.

You plan your death from this side, creating a set of beliefs and stories that you'll live out. All those convoluted beliefs about hell and burning fires create a whole drama for you of your own making. If you decide that death is a deliverance, that you will be once again the true you, be one with your higher self, be the best version of yourself, be perfect and all knowing and all wise, then that will be so. Prepare for it now.

This lifetime is one such small part of our existence. Some lives are designed to be just hours long. Whatever it is, it is appropriate. It causes huge grief, but it is appropriate.

I think that's enough for now.

Cool, eh, Mom?

Very cool.

CHAPTER 6

So, you call it pushing the reset button. I call it stepping out. I like your term even better because it connotes a deliberate act. And to find us, you look for our light.

Yup. It's easy. Brighter than a flashlight, some of you shine.

Really?

Then to get you to hear us, we use all kinds of techniques: music, animals, electronics, smell, language. With language, we start by repetition—the same thing, the same phrase, over and over. Drives us a bit crazy, but some of you finally stop and notice. I kept making the suggestion of looking at the lamp over and over so that you would feel there was a significant message associated with it.

The funny thing is we figure it is such an incredible feat to bridge this divide, and we figure you're going to tell us something earth-shattering when communication is made. What do you actually say? "I love you." Makes you wonder …

Three words that make magic.

Clo, some might see your life as tragedy, but I see it as perfection. You chose a most difficult, contentious route, pissing everyone off, stealing, lying, cheating, using and even prostituting yourself to get your fix. You tried to alienate the ones who loved you, and you sought out the dealers and the users and the abuse.

You didn't do it 70, 80, or 90 percent. You did it all the way. Remember Kenora?

Painful.

It was early February 2009. You had decided the previous Christmas to sell your belongings and travel. Then I get the call. An anonymous female voice tells me you've been victimized and abused, and you are in a rundown hotel in a town called Kenora, Ontario.

The closest airport to Kenora is Winnipeg, so I fly to Winnipeg, arriving at 9:00 p.m. The drive to Kenora should take about two and a half hours. It takes me five. It's minus 40 with howling winds, blistering whiteouts and one snowy lane on a pitch-black Trans-Canada Highway. I make it, driven by a mother's deep love and heart-stopping, mind-numbing worry. My little Kia rental is frozen solid, literally shaking. I am too.

Frozen or shaking?

Both. This isn't funny. Don't distract me.

I pull into town about 2:00 a.m. and see a running police car. Sergeant White is somewhat alarmed to see me, but he quickly rallies. Together we find the run-down motel.

To this day, Sergeant White is my real-life hero. He's built like a sub-zero refrigerator with the heart of a good, kind man. He's exactly what I need.

The woman behind the desk refuses to tell us which room you're in. I threaten to break down every door. She looks at me and looks at my companion. Calling the police wouldn't do much good. Sergeant White agrees that he'll go in and check on you—no broken doors, no commotion. It almost kills me to not be able to enter your room.

"She's in rough shape," he says. "But she's alive and has agreed to come with me to the hospital tomorrow at 9:00 a.m. I'll be back at 9:00."

I hug him.

The wicked witch behind the counter rents me a room for 95 dollars. It's almost 4:00 a.m. I never take off my coat or boots. I sleep for 14 minutes on top of the yucky bedspread. The morning dawns sunny and terribly cold. I thought I knew cold, but this was a whole different level of freezing. By 9:00 a.m. Sergeant White is back.

Clo, what an odyssey that became. What a mess you were emotionally, psychologically and physically. I aged many years that day. The psych staff at Lake of the Woods District Hospital were kind and agreed to keep you as long as you wanted to stay. From my room at the Super 8 across the way, I could gaze over at the hospital and imagine you sleeping peacefully, protected and cared for. I was actually able to have some blessed sleep. I stayed a week.

You stayed two weeks then went AWOL. When the doctor called me to say you'd disappeared, I was at a Toronto trade show, manning my booth.

"I think you'd better sit down," he said.

I sat.

"She's pregnant."

I had to go back to my booth and pass out granola samples when what I really felt like doing was passing out—or better yet, leaving the trade show and going to look for you. Again.

I was frantic to find you. You managed somehow to make it to Winnipeg and get arrested. I was thankful for that; at least you had a warm bed and three meals. Imagine: I'm thankful that you're in a detention centre. Everything is relative. I used to be glad when you got *A*s in school.

A lawyer is hired and we wait for a decision. By now you're almost 20 weeks pregnant. I'm panicking. Your dad brings you back into town. The abortion is done. Another drama is over. Time to heal.

Chloe 2yrs old

Chloe 18yrs old

Chloe, when I look at the essence of you, I see beauty and perfection, a being who dedicates itself to teaching through suffering. Your terrible acts were designed to bring out the best in us. Sometimes it worked, and sometimes I wasn't up to the task.

Today, I connect the dots. You were our catalyst to help us examine our beliefs, to get honest with ourselves, to love you in spite of yourself. Today, I can say I succeeded because you stuck with the program. You made yourself contrary. You made yourself ornery, difficult, mean, rude and abusive—all manner of things designed to push me away. Before I understood, those actions did push me away. And then I realized what a teacher you are and what a gift you are in all our lives. I love you in spite of yourself. Thank you. You taught me to go beyond the physical, to see your perfect essence and thereby know a level of love and acceptance I had not previously known.

You were not concerned with social niceties. You were not concerned with manners, with appearances, with gratitude or appreciation of any of it. You were obsessed. You stayed obsessed right till the end, and you pushed. I learned to love you in spite of all that. You taught me to love.

I wanted so much to give you a "beautiful death," a peaceful end to a tumultuous life.

When you first were hospitalized, they didn't realize how sick you were. You had scurvy. Scurvy! Your body was severely bloated. The medical staff had no idea what was going on. They were treating that mysterious body rash with ointments when it was a symptom of severe malnutrition. It had been weeks since you'd eaten properly because of the blockage in your colon.

You came back from the verge of stepping out of your body to regain enough physical stamina to have operations and treatments. You had chances to go swimming and kayaking again, to walk in the countryside, to take hours and hours of country road drives, to play cards, to paint, to cook, to shop, to smile and, even on a couple of occasions, to dance.

We did, Mom. We did.

And only when you were ready, you decided to leave the dream that is this physical reality and merge back into your true self.

I'm excited for you, excited about all the possibilities ahead for you. So many choices. I know now that they are always wise ones, no matter what they are.

As you went through the process of conscious dying, you ushered in my conscious development of parenting. It was conscious, not sudden. It was often painful and sometimes blessed. You set the pace.

I had to forego all agenda-making in favour of allowing. I couldn't control the situation, just as I couldn't stop the cancer from progressing. So I let go of wanting a different life for you, choosing instead to take my cues from you.

"Eat dessert first," a metaphor for beginning with the end in mind, was how we lived every day. We knew the end would come; we were aware of the body's increasing struggle. Habits and routines were dropped when they became too cumbersome or complex, and life became simpler and simpler, losing none of its essence of value even while marching towards the palliative care hospital room towards the very end.

It was always blessed. It was never easy. It was a gift. That was the key—to look for the gifts.

I'm reading a great book, *The Conscious Parent* by Shefali Tsabary. On page 20 she writes, "Using the present moment as a living laboratory, everyday interactions have the potential to teach invaluable lessons." Boy, does that ever apply when accompanying a child towards her stepping out from the body!

I deliberately rename death stepping out because it is a natural deliberate move out of physical space into free space, like that Friday night of stepping out to the nightclub, where I went from a constrained human being to a free spirit on the dance floor.

You helped me realize what it is to be a conscious parent, loving your essence and your better self when the exterior behaviour you were manifesting was completely chaotic and crazy. I had to look beyond that craziness, knowing it was an illness talking; it wasn't Chloe. Chloe was an act of God both in the sense that she was an uncontrollable, unpredictable disaster as well as a divine being living a human experience. She was both. We are all both, and you reminded me of this often.

Tsabary suggests taking the time every day to ask yourself if you really know who your children are, because who they are is ever changing, ever evolving. Who even thinks of stuff like that while we're trying to pay bills, fold laundry, do groceries, cook dinner and finish a science project before bedtime? How enlightened yet utterly inconceivable within the confines of a single mother's hectic day. It just ain't gonna happen.

One of your greatest teachings was helping me let go of my ego in relation to status, acceptability, perfection and accomplishment. Every hope and wish I held for you was dashed. You did the opposite—pushed every button, broke every rule, defied every limit.

On page 48, Tsabary writes, "Letting go of your attachment to your vision of parenthood and your desire to write your children's future is the hardest psychic death to endure."

I would like to elaborate that the actual death of a child is about the letting go of the dreams and hopes you held for her since she was a newborn in your arms. No, since she was in the womb. She has no future, only a present. And therein lies the present, the gift. Accepting that the divine plan is correct and just—even when things seem unfair in our three-dimensional world—is the hardest task of all.

Or is it?

Even something as devastating as the death of a child can be seen different ways, depending on your beliefs. My experience with matters of life and death has shown me irrefutable proof that there is only life after life, that the stepping out of this body leads to freedom and choice. It is now, while we assume these heavy physical bodies, that we are burdened. We are separate and are searching constantly for reconnection and oneness. Once we've stepped out of this life, we reconnect, like waking up from a dream.

Life after death is a self-fulfilling arena. If one imagines that it will be a bed of roses, that is what one will transition to. If one holds the belief that loved ones will be there to greet us, they will be there. There is choice, there is healing, there is continuous possibility and especially, there is growth. It doesn't sound anything like dying. It actually sounds like being very much alive. And the truth is that it is.

It was January 31. I remember heading out of town, just a couple of weeks before you stepped out, for one day and night to myself. I hoped to catch up on some sleep. I needed solitude and a hot bath.

At 3:49 a.m., the phone rang. It was you, distraught. "Mom, could you make me some green tea?" Again at 6:30 a.m. you called. "Mom, I think I was born incoherent."

I'll never forget that one.

You were reflecting and searching for some peace. How to help you feel some peace? The only thing that made sense was to model the feeling, so I decided to deliberately be peaceful. Full stop.

CHAPTER 7

Mom, Kid, whatever, I can see you've had several experiences communicating with this consciousness. Some are recorded. All these dots are connecting now. What happened?

You want to know?

I want to know.

I'll tell you what happened. First, do you believe me when I say I won't exaggerate or invent any part of it?

I believe you.

No invention. No exaggeration. In fact, you can't imagine how relieved I am to be able to share this. I've been hanging on to these writings for years.

Tell me, already!

Okay. I always felt that I was receiving nudges from the other side. Back in 1994, I was washing the kitchen floor, and I heard the voice of my favourite Motown singer, Marvin Gaye, in my head.

Marvin Gaye?

Yup. He said to me, "Andrea, I want you to know that I chose the manner of my death. My music was created to illustrate my values of life, my love for my brothers, my belief that peace is the answer. What better way to illustrate the irony of a world gone mad than to be killed by a bullet from a gun in my father's hand?"

How'd you know it was him?

That thought came to me fully formed, and it kept repeating itself till I stopped and acknowledged it. It was like a loudspeaker that spoke to me in my head. I simply knew. Then he was gone.

That was it?

That day, that was it. Small stuff like that happened on and off over the years, but Marvin is the one I remember best. Then in 2010, I was reading a biography of Abraham Lincoln, *Team of Rivals* by Doris Kearns Goodwin. One morning as I was heading to work, something told me not to go. I'd never missed work, so this was a big thing for me to stay home.

That's the truth.

I kept hearing this one phrase repeating itself over and over in my head: "My error was not in underestimating the value of my words at Gettysburg." It almost made no sense to me—kinda like "objects in the mirror are closer than they appear." (I know that's one of your favourites.)

Ah, it is. But you digress, Madam.

Okay, okay. Gettysburg meant just one person to me: Abraham Lincoln. Also, the phrase wasn't coming from me. It was only half a thought, and so I decided to see what would happen if I made some space for the rest of the thought to come through so that the idea would be complete.

I sat down with a pen and paper and began writing. I took down thousands of words without hesitation. It took several days to write. I still have the paper version of it, and there isn't a correction or a hesitation.

It's time to share it.

I wrote thousands and thousands of inspired words from Abraham Lincoln. Then Franklin Delano Roosevelt, Eleanor Roosevelt and Queen Victoria. I remember the first phrase she repeated in my head was, "I have but one goal at the moment: to abandon the imposition of order." There were others too. Amy Winehouse, Theo Van Gogh, Michelangelo, Che Guevara.

I wanted to include them as an appendix to this conversation and finally share them with more people than just a few close friends. Whatever people will think, at least the material would have the chance to be read. It can be disputed, discounted or ridiculed, but I believe the vibration of the words will touch people who are open enough to believe without seeing. I took their words down as I received them and felt extremely honoured and touched to do so. I still do.

I doubt many things in my life, but not the validity of those writings.

Doubt is deliberate destruction of self-confidence. Doubt is the bulldozer of life. You were going to include them but didn't. Why?

Too long—another 10,000 words. It took centuries in some cases for those words to find the light of day. I know the proper vehicle will present itself.

No doubt there.

Listen to this coincidence, Clo. You know how I never watch TV. I haven't owned a TV in years, and left to my own devices, I would never turn on a TV. I've been living in John's cottage for three months and have never turned on my TV.

Yesterday afternoon, we're relaxing at my place, and he turns on the TV. Who do I see? The curator from the Lincoln Museum in Springfield, Illinois, talking about art fraud. His name is James Cornelius. John looks at me. Just minutes before, we had been discussing the material, and John had suggested I get in touch with the curator from the Lincoln Museum.

You felt that nudge loud and clear!

We both did. This morning, I sent Cornelius an email. We'll see what he responds.

Very cool, Mom. You kept this to yourself for six years? Why didn't you try to publish it? To send it to the Lincoln museum or get it out somehow?

I was afraid of criticism from others. I was afraid to be in a position where I was defending this incredible material and, in so doing, would cause the message to be belittled or reduced. I know what I know, but I didn't feel I wanted to defend anything.

I sent it to my mother and a few friends, but that's it. I felt I had let Lincoln down by not sharing it with a wider audience. It was like he'd trusted me with this material, and I did nothing of value with it.

That's heavy. Enough. Think of the lamp shade.

That's how I felt. It was one more dot connecting a whole lot of different experiences that kept confirming there is no death, there is no death. Only I couldn't share this new knowing with anyone.

I was writing articles for a newspaper at the time and sent it in to my editor. "Fascinating," she said. "Keep writing." That was it. Two years after starting, the writings stopped. I thought perhaps it was my doing because I hadn't honoured the work enough, hadn't made a bigger effort to make it public.

The value is in the words themselves. While reading them, I feel the resonance of truth. That's all you have to do, Mom. Put them out there and leave the rest up to the Divine. Just trust, Ma.

I'm trying.

I'm tickling your cheek. Feel it? Is it bugging you yet?

It's bugging me. You're such a brat. Sentimental moment is over.

One of the writings, the story by Eleanor Roosevelt, incorporated something I had written years before. That really made me wonder about how every thought is known, every action is known. There is really nothing hidden, although we seem to think we can hide our secret selves from others.

There are no secrets.

I remember thinking that at the time. The strange thing about this one is she incorporates a thought I had years ago about "The 10 past 10."

What's the 10 past 10?

Years ago, back when I was working with your father—so it must have been around 1994—I was looking at a magazine and noticed how the watch advertisements all had the hands of the watches at 10 past 10. One after another, the hands were placed at 10 past 10.

I thought, *Interesting how time stands still at 10 past 10.* I started glancing at the clock at exactly 10:10 every day. I trained myself to stop and take a moment to show gratitude at that moment, and 10 past 10 became the present moment. The Now. It was a really nice ritual, stopping at a precise moment every day to acknowledge and give thanks.

From there I extrapolated the 11:11, which is the past. November 11, Remembrance Day. And 12:12 is the future.

So the 10:10, the 11:11 and the 12:12 are the present, the past and the future. We can show gratitude for one, acceptance of the other and allowing of the third. Nice.

That's the perfect summary, Clo. One of the writings mentioned the 10:10, and I thought, *Gee, is it possible that she's incorporating some of my thoughts into her thoughts? Is it possible to have any original thoughts, or are all thoughts just shared between all of us in one giant cosmic soup?*

What would you label as an original thought? Something you haven't heard before?

Exactly.

Just because you haven't heard it doesn't mean it hasn't been said elsewhere. Once it is expressed, it becomes part of collective consciousness and can be accessed by the collective. The collective is a massive tree of all human life.

Ask Daniel about some of this. He knows there is an even more massive tree that includes non-human life—animal, vegetable, mineral. He knows the trees talk, the crickets ground energy on the planet. He knows about the vibration of molecules and matter considered to be inanimate. All is animate. Animate. Animal. Animam.

Had to look that one up. *Animam* is Latin for "soul." Very cool, Clo.

Mom, there is a ton of super cool stuff going on every second of the day. We're all being constantly offered the opportunity to choose higher. To help us, we access that collective consciousness, especially during sleep. It's especially during sleep that this type of thought and knowledge is accessed.

You're a great teacher. Who knew?

Once I realized the difference between my thoughts and a totally foreign thought—which was actually not so difficult because they were so different in tone and content—that one first phrase, the prompt, acted like a catalyst to open the door. Then all the other words started to tumble out, one after another. I didn't feel like I was dreaming or in some kind of altered state. I just felt like I was listening and recording.

Conversing with you is not quite the same. The familiarity makes for a conversation that's totally normal—with one exception. I can't see you. And I'm not used to you being so coherent.

From this side, using one phrase to get your attention is a common strategy. Also, if we're too frazzled and nervous, we won't come through clearly. If we're impatient to connect or too emotional, the signal is garbled. It takes a lightness, patience, persistence and strong intent to connect across the divide. In your case, as the receiver, it simply takes an openness to receive.

Wouldn't it be cool, Clo, if we could train ourselves to be better senders and receivers so that when we cross over, we can communicate easily with loved ones on a more normal basis? It wouldn't be some weird paranormal event. It would simply be the continuation of life and of the relationships we treasure. Imagine how real the conversation could get!

We could call it the School of Thought—how to project and retrieve thoughts across the veil. Neat. Another project for you, Mom.

No shortage of those, Clo.

So you have all these writings. You sit on them. And then what?

And then you cross over, press reset, and give me the courage to let people know that there is no death. That it is possible to talk across this divide, and that it's not the huge divide that we all think it is.

In fact, I'd venture to guess that many people carry on these types of conversations with their loved ones, but they don't let others know for fear of ridicule and judgement.

I guess I'm at the point where I can truly say, "To hell with worrying any more about what everyone will think. This is what's happening. This is the reality of life." This conversation is real, and even though I'm still afraid to offer it up to others, I'm also being pushed by you and others to do so. To not do so would be to turn my back on all the events that led up to this moment, most specifically the events of December 1991.

December 1991? I was 3 years old.

A lovely, magnificent little thing. I have some great shots of you at that age.

You're getting sidetracked again. Back to December 1991. I can see the event.

You can see it?

There are no secrets, Mom.

You've told me that already.

You need reminding. All the basics need reminding and reinforcing. The rudiments. The fundaments. The filament. The firmament.

I love the way you toss words around, like a juggler.

That's Uncle Al's specialty. Remember how he used to entertain us? I loved him for that.

Me too. He's your godfather, but you didn't get much of him.

Not enough, anyway. That was my turn to digress. I can speak to Uncle Al in his dreams. Now that's quality time.

You've gotta tell me more about that.

You've gotta tell me about December 1991. It was life-changing.

It was. I kept this to myself for 25 years and finally told it in full this past March.

I went to Vancouver to visit Sue after your funeral was done. I'm fooling around online, and up pops the IANDS website address. IANDS stands for International Association for Near Death Studies. A quick email to reach out, a return email the following day, and we agree to meet to discuss my near death experience. What a gift! To be listened to without scepticism or interruption. The session is taped and later transcribed. Here it is.

It was December of 1991. It was a special day because it was the day of my Grandmother Emily's funeral.

How old was she when she died?

Ninety-two. I woke up that morning and had a vision as I woke of me and your dad being hit by a car. I saw the make and colour of the car. I saw the snowy, stormy night. I heard him scream. I debated how would it be possible for two people walking on a sidewalk to be hit.

The difference between a dream and a vision is that with a dream, the details fade. With a vision, the details remain.

Then I got on with my day and attended my grandmother's funeral. I was close to Grandma when I was growing up. She was very connected to plants and nature, to nurturing a healthy mind and body. We were two peas in a pod.

The funeral went fine. As we were leaving the chapel, I met Marjorie Greevy, Grandma's close friend. Grandma had spoken of her often with such affection and friendship. I introduced myself and offered to give her a ride home, and that's how I met wonderful Marjorie.

I remember going to see Marjorie in the hospital right before she died. She is so fit, Mom. You should see her now. She keeps telling me it's the dancing, it's the music. Keep dancing, she's telling you.

Thanks, Marjorie. When I ask myself what's the one thing that always makes me happy, it's dancing, and I don't do enough of it. Thanks for the reminder.

That same evening, your dad and I had to make an appearance at a Christmas party given by our priest. Because your dad was involved with the church, we felt obliged to attend, but I was completely exhausted.

The priest's home sat up on a hill on a large, curved boulevard that banked down towards the right just in front of his house. It was snowing heavily, a real December blizzard with howling winds and huge snowflakes being whipped around. Visibility was terrible and snowbanks were high. The roads were a slippery mess.

There were cars parked in every available spot with only small openings left for driveways.

At 10:00 p.m., we left the party. As we walked east on the snowy sidewalk, we were hit by a car heading east, down the hill. It had managed to jump the curb at the perfect moment to pass between a small opening in the parked cars, where there was a single driveway. It hit us from behind. The timing was impeccable. We never saw it coming.

That morning's vision came back to me. I heard your dad scream the exact words he had said in exactly the same intonation. As I'm flying through the air, I realized I'd been forewarned, and there was no need to panic. I hit a parked car with the left side of my head, hit the pavement and slid about 35 feet down the road. No other cars hit me. Your dad flipped backwards over the car, shattered the windshield, and landed in the snow.

That's when the near-death experience happened. I literally floated out of my body, hovering about seven feet above it. I observed it lying on the ground, but at first I didn't realize that my consciousness had separated from my physical self. I tried to talk to people. They couldn't hear me. Yet I could see the whole scene.

I saw the partygoers spill out of the house. The police, the ambulance, the priest, everyone screaming. I saw the car. It was the exact colour and make I had seen in my vision that morning. I saw your dad and the female driver crouched over my body. She was hysterical.

I felt absolutely no pain. I was concerned for all those ladies in their Christmas finery out in a snowstorm with no coats on.

Then I gradually moved away from the scene as I was drawn into a magnificent, warm light. It was filled with love, Clo. Filled with love! Words can't capture the feeling. I was enveloped in light and love and was greeted by a tall figure. I couldn't make out distinct features but the presence seemed male to me.

He addressed me by name. I remember thinking, "You know my name?"

To this day, I reflect on how I was blown away by being addressed by name, as if I didn't think I deserved such divine attention. It still causes me to pause and think about my sense of self-worth. Anyhow, I digress again.

You digress again and again. Back to the story already.

It's not a story, Clo. It's what happened, with no exaggeration or embellishment.

You're just trying to use fancy words with double letters.

Now you're digressing.

That incredible being of light spoke to me. "Andrea," he said, "you can stay with us or you can go back. What do you choose?"

I didn't reflect long before answering. I was thinking of my three babies at home, and my answer came quickly. "I have to go back", I said. "Even if every bone is broken, I have to go back."

He asked me again in a firm, calm voice.

"Yes, I'm sure. I have to go back."

The moment I gave that second response, I felt myself slide into this swirling vortex. It was circular, like water going down a drain. A powerful, swirling motion gripped me. I had to use all my focus to stay with it. Moments later, I felt myself slam back into my body with a terrific jolt. I woke up crying.

The first person I saw when I awoke was the priest. He was crouched over me and had me in his arms. "Andrea," he said, "your Grandma Emily is with you tonight, and I know she had a hand in saving you."

He was correct.

Yes, he was, Clo.

While immobilized with a neck brace, strapped into a stretcher, and placed side by side in the same ambulance as your dad, I thought, *Something or someone has gone to a lot of trouble to prepare me for this. How is it possible that a warning—complete with the colour and make of the car, the storm and his scream—was given to me this morning? And then to be offered the choice to stay or to go?*

I was given a glimpse into another time-space reality. I had read that linear time is a construct of this three-dimensional world, but I'd never really understood what that meant. Now, I had experienced this warping of time first-hand. And that love, Clo, that all-encompassing divine white light of love, showed me that death is a return to love and that my life matters.

I made two vows to myself right there during that short ambulance ride to the hospital. I decided I would not live any longer in a bad marriage without love. I also decided that I was going to make my life count.

It took a near-death experience to make you realize two obvious conclusions? Anyone could know those without getting the shit knocked out of her.

Anyone else, maybe, but not me. I had accepted that marriage is "till death do us part."

You did die, Mom.

You're right, actually. I never thought of it that way. I simply thought that I had to make my life matter because it had mattered enough to others. It had mattered enough that they gave me the warning, the near-death experience.

A small correction. It wasn't a near-death experience. It was a death experience.

And your body?

My whole body went black and blue, but miraculously not one bone was broken for either of us. An amazing, incredible miracle.

I had a run in my stockings. My head hurt from hitting the parked car. The place of impact, my right calf, hurt for 20 years, more as a reminder than anything else.

A reminder of what?

A reminder to not squander my life doing insignificant things. A reminder that every life counts. That we all matter. That what we choose and how we execute those choices matter. That we are not alone. That we are loved and cared for and that there is so much more going on than meets the eye. It's a reminder to believe in miracles.

Do you?

Completely. This is one right now.

Mom, this is a conversation. You're getting melodramatic. It bridges the gap, but it's not a miracle. It's more common than people realize, and it's going to be documented more and more.

It may not seem like a miracle to you, but it is to me. To be able to talk with you like this, to hear you speak so coherently, to hear you period. It's a miracle to me.

Okay, okay. Back to the accident.

Are all conversations this full of side roads and detours?

Grandma used to tell me every woman should own a red coat. That night, I had on my heavy, long red winter coat. Although it became embedded with shattered glass, that coat acted like a shield, protecting me. I didn't even have one cut on my skin. I used crutches for a few days and then tossed those aside. Incredible.

For several months, my mother came over and rubbed my badly bruised body with castor oil. That castor oil, plus all the yoga, stretching, exercising and physio, healed me. Hot baths with Epsom salts helped too. I have to be careful with my back, but I'm just fine. The only thing I can't do is carry a 50-pound knapsack on my back. But who wants to do that anyway?

My hair instantly went grey from the shock. I didn't realize that for about two weeks. It also took me two weeks to work up the courage to ask your dad to leave. He agreed to go.

I was only 3, but I remember the five of us sitting on the sofa. There was something really solemn and really grown-up about the mood. I remember hearing your announcement that you were separating and feeling that something big had happened.

The fact that I remember it so perfectly speaks volumes about how we treat children when there are big announcements to make, like the death of a parent. Even if they don't understand, children should be told what has happened in simple language. They'll be able to process things better later if they hear the simple truth. Hiding it from them messes them up.

It was the ending of one life and the beginning of another. The grounds for divorce were adultery. There was no argument.

CHAPTER 8

Very gradually, after that event, I began to feel my Grandmother Emily with me.

I first noticed it because she had the worst table manners. She had lived on her own for so many years, and she had let good manners slip away. It was embarrassing sometimes when I was with her. She would make these huge burps. And she chewed her food like … well, it was like a horse chewing. She would forego the cutlery and eat with her hands. I started doing the same thing.

And you thought I had bad table manners!

You did have terrible table manners. Time spent homeless on the streets and scrounging for food had made you somewhat savage, like you had forgotten your upbringing.

I remember taking you to a restaurant up north last summer. You opened a small packet of peanut butter, picked up your knife and proceeded to use the blade to scoop up the peanut butter into your mouth. You polished off the whole thing. I also remember you sticking your face right down into your plate and shovelling the food in your mouth, as opposed to using your fork and …

Okay, okay. Stop. I get the picture. Can we get back to Grandma?

Grandma. Yup. First I started making these huge burps. I would catch myself eating with my hands, all sloppy and messy just like her, and chewing my food with my mouth open and food falling out. It was like I had lost all my manners. I had to catch myself. It was so unlike me that I realized she was somehow with me.

Then I started hearing her talking to me in my head.

Voices in your head? No kidding.

No kidding. I heard her, clear as a bell. It was subtle at first. It used to strike me that the voices you heard and the voices I heard were just a fine line away from each other. Why are you branded crazy and I am intuitive?

Mom, the voices in my head were not helpful. They were destructive, harassing and abusive. Who would do that to themselves? You could listen and record but not react to the voices you heard. I was powerless against them.

Such a subtle yet huge difference of the origin and value. Yet people constantly hear voices in their heads. I used to think that if you could have controlled your reaction to them, keeping your conversation silent much as I did, you would never have been branded psychotic.

In my case, they overtook not just my mind but my body as well. It was like I had sold my soul to the devil. I made a pact with the entity that possessed me, and that agreement ended only when my body was incinerated. Thank God that's over.

People should know that drugs can rip open the protective armour, the aura around the body. Physical abuse can have the same effect. A fall, a strong hit on the football field, a punch, any invasion to the body can create a rip that renders the physical form vulnerable to possession. That's what it is: possession.

I used to think you were possessed. I had even tried to find a priest at one point, to exorcise you.

It wouldn't have worked because of the pact I made with the entity.

I feel sick when I think that others are going through this, and we aren't able to properly help them. What can they do, Clo?

Don't do drugs of any kind. Meds or drugs. Weed is not recreation. Weed is desecration.

Be kinder to the body to avoid ripping the aura. Protect yourself better by encircling the body with white divine light before interaction at a cocktail party, the mall, a car dealership or a football game (whether playing or spectating). Protect the self. The one thing that makes these entities uncomfortable is love.

I will attempt to explain in terms you can comprehend. Many entities wish to remain in human form. In doing so, they don't need to progress or heal or grow. They eventually will, because all souls eventually move along their paths, but they can way delay the process by clinging close to your plane of consciousness and piggybacking or possessing a human form.

First, there needs to be an opening in the human aura for the entity to latch on. This can happen in many ways. It can be trauma in the birth canal during birth. It can be a sports injury, especially one to the head. It can be from drug use, which destabilizes the body's defences against possession. Beware of recreational drugs. It can be simply that the entity is already with the human from other lifetimes, and the mission is not yet complete.

Possession is as real as your nose, as real as the sun rising each day. Possession comprises two parties that collaborate on some level. It's hard to believe that such a dynamic is collaborative, but it is. In my case, I both hated and loved my possessor. I could not extricate myself, and neither did I often want to. Sometimes I came close to wanting to, especially when I had been well for some time. I began making plans and envisaging a life, but the hold was too strong. I couldn't get it to let go. So I gave up and gave in. I didn't sell my soul, as the popular media likes to call it. I loaned it out. That lease has now expired.

Funny how the word *expired* is used to indicate the end of a term of contract and death. Can a perfectly normal human being become possessed without warning?

Yes. However, this is rare because the human will reject the thoughts of the entity, reject the destructiveness and the rage in favour of healing and wellness. She will, in fact, do everything she can to get rid of the entity. Because entities want to latch on, they go to the lowest-hanging fruit, so to speak. It's easier to latch on to someone who is wide open and vulnerable rather than to someone who is solid, grounded and healthy in their body, mind and spirit. They are attracted to those who are less healthy, less grounded and vulnerable. They look for humans with less integrity of mind as well. Those who will shoplift, cheat on an exam, steal from their mother's purse, kick a dog, spend their inheritance on drugs or walk out of the exam room before completing the test, thereby flunking out and sinking into denial and despair. Emotions such as hopelessness and despair go a long way to assisting these entities to find homes on earth.

We'll explore this concept in more detail later. For now, back to Grandma.

Back to Grandma. Did you know she was 92 when she died?

You told me that already. Other than her age, I know almost nothing about her, Mom. I know she made great granola. That's all I know. And I know she looks great now.

She lived by herself. My grandfather had died three decades earlier. Grandma was a pioneer of healthy eating. She would eat a bowl of cherries for a meal. Flaxseed tea, sprouts growing on the windowsill, three almonds a day, juicing, wonderful hugs and her long hair braided and coiled neatly around her head—this is what I remember most. I was fascinated by that braid. At the end of her life, in the interest of practicality, it was cut off. That made me sad.

My grandparents had come by boat from Syria as young children to start a new life in the new world. They met here, married and had four daughters and one son. My mother, Granny Adele, is her youngest. Grandma had a garden in the back where she grew some of the vegetables she juiced. She was like no one else I knew: strong, independent and not concerned with fitting into societal norms.

Sounds like someone else I know.

Do you know when I'm smiling?

If I tune in, I can feel everything you feel.

Then you know I'm smiling now.

Yup.

Grandma always had fresh juice waiting for us when we went over. Her favourite was carrot and dandelion. She insisted we drink it. Yuck—it tasted strong and bitter. The bitterer, the better. We didn't argue with Grandma.

The errors that your Grandma Emily made with her daughter, my Granny Adele, are being corrected with you. The errors you and I made are being righted as we speak. We're all constantly seeking absolution, and it is constantly being granted. But guess who grants it to us? We do. God is within.

That's a fascinating subject—how we remove obstacles from future generations by making choices from a place of forgiveness, atonement and highest good. We literally change the future. We could talk about that all day. But you want to know more about Grandma, right?

Right.

Okay. My Grandmother Emily was a force in my life, and a force in everyone's life. She was opinionated, strong-willed and tough. She spent the last few weeks of her life in a hospital bed in the foetal position. The only part of her body that moved was one finger. One finger.

Her eyes gazed at us with a clear, fierce vision. And that finger. She would wave and wag it. I could feel she was impatient to leave that broken body.

About two months after her funeral, I heard her say, "Andrea, go get my books. They're in Lillian's basement in a box. I want you to start reading them."

I wanted to ask a ton of questions, but she was gone.

I called up my mother, and sure enough, there was a box of Grandma's stuff in her sister Lillian's basement. The books are a series of small volumes, numbered one through five and entitled *The Life and Teachings of the Masters of the Far East*. The hard covers are worn, weathered, and full of Grandma's notes and scribbles. Phrases are underlined. Margins are a mess of comments, pencilled and penned in. I did attempt to read them, but their meaning eluded me. Back they went into the box for about two years.

She's telling me she had to have patience with you. You were stubborn and hard-headed. And you had that totally annoying habit of always doubting yourself.

Even now she's practicing patience. She's staying out of this even though she has so much to say. She's telling me we get sidetracked enough as it is. If she entered this conversation, we'd never get the important material out.

What is the important material, Clo? Is it the information about death? Is it the near-death experience? Is it the tools I used to make it through so much chaos?

No, silly. It's this conversation. The very fact that it's happening, that it is. You are. I am. Period. That is the important event. That is the seed to bring hope to others that death is not an end. That is the end to this method and means. That is the mission we are intended to complete. When it is done, I will move on.

So you stayed close in order to write this book together?

Sometimes you are so slow.

I get sidetracked. I wander. I meander.

Don't we all. Grandma …

My grandmother was always considered a bit eccentric. She believed so much in juicing that she used to buy juicing machines and give them to her friends. Those machines weren't cheap; they were hundreds of dollars, and she lived on a very tight budget. Yet she managed to find the money to buy people juicing machines to help them stay healthy. "Food as medicine" was her mantra.

I know what it is to take medicine as food.

Did you ever. I have a few pictures to prove it.

She travelled by herself. I remember taking her to the airport in the fall for her flight down south. For many years, she spent the winter in a small, rented room on Collins Avenue in Miami Beach. She'd walk through the airport with her shopping bag full of half-sprouted plants.

That wouldn't fly today.

That's for sure. Can't go to the States with a clementine. Imagine a shopping bag full of live plants!

I remember visiting her in Florida and wanting to bring her home with me. I didn't like her being there all by herself. At that time, the area was shabby and run-down. I worried about her because I loved her. When she was too ill to come to family dinners, I fretted and wanted to go spend the evening with her, rather than sit casually around the dining room table as if all was well.

There were occasions when Grandma would stay over at our

house. She used to sleep on the dining room floor, preferring that to a bed. One night I watched, enthralled, as she uncoiled her hair. That braid was almost to her waist.

When she was fed up with the nuisance of heavy, droopy breasts that hurt her back, she had breast-reduction surgery at 72 years of age. Was she ever proud to show them to me! They were awesome, Clo. Like the breasts of a 19-year-old.

I wish!

Fast forward to the fall of 1992. My mother called to say they had finalized Grandma's estate. Her final wishes were fulfilled, and there was a small balance left in her account. My mother felt I should have it. It was exactly the same amount as the lawyer's bill I had just received to pay for my divorce.

"Thank you, Grandma," I sobbed as I stood at the automatic banking machine.

A couple of years later, I picked up her books again. "When the student is ready, the teacher appears." This time, the material did not disappoint. It changed me. I learned so many fundamentals about life and what is really going on. Then around 1996, Grandma began talking to me again.

"We're going to learn patience," she'd say. Then another time it would be tolerance. Then forgiveness. Acceptance. Authenticity. She was like my tutor. I'd wake up in bed and she'd be talking to me clear as day.

One time—only one time—I saw her. I was driving on the highway and I saw her face looking straight at me in my windshield. There was an enormous light behind her head. I almost went off the road.

That was a great gift.

And a great shock.

Around the same time, I'm watering the plants in my parents' apartment, and Grandma says to me, "Go in the den and get the picture at the bottom of the bookcase."

I go in the den, and sure enough, there's this nice photo that had been taken at my sister's wedding.

"Take the picture and go make a label."

"A what?"

"We're going into business," she says. Seriously. This is exactly how it happened. No business plan. No market research. Just Grandma saying, "Go make a label."

"What are we going to do?" I ask.

"We're going to make granola," she says. You don't argue with Grandma. I had a logo designed, and the label was made. We did go into business, and the company was called Grandma Emily's Granola.

CHAPTER 9

And then what happened?

What happened? Nothing happened. I had absolutely no idea how to start. I had no plan, no money, no experience with making food commercially. I had spent 250 precious dollars to make a logo from a photograph. That was it.

What actually happened is that your dad put his company into bankruptcy and declared personal bankruptcy as well. Even though we had been divorced almost five years, I was still working for him. I figured putting my lot in with his was the smartest way to ensure the future for my children. Wrong. One fine spring day, I lost my job and all child support payments. Then we were saved by a cat.

Saved by Max.

Yup. Just as I'm putting you guys to bed one night, I hear a small noise at our front door. I open the door, and in runs this tiny kitten. Everyone goes ballistic. Daniel pulls the card that the next day is his birthday. "Mom, we have to keep the cat."

I'm wondering if it belongs to someone else, even though it has no collar on. I put it back outside. "If it's there in the morning, we'll keep the cat."

You put the cat back outside?

It was June, and it was warm. Not like it was February or something.

Okay, okay.

Sure enough, after a sleepless night, I open the door, and in runs the cat. Everyone is thrilled. Off we go to the vet, cat in a shoebox, to make sure it's healthy. That's where I meet Sara, a woman I know casually from an exercise class. Sara explains that she's involved in a new organization to raise awareness for breast cancer. They're putting on a breakfast event and need some interesting morning fare, something out of the ordinary. I offer my granola, thinking I'll be supplying my product to 10 women sitting around a table. I happen to have a jar in my car because I was delivering some to a friend that day. I specifically remember putting the shoebox down and heading to the car for that jar.

Three days later, Sara calls to tell me they would love to have the granola at their event. "Ticket sales are encouraging. We're expecting a thousand people."

What? First I panic. Then I call my mother.

When the shit hits, call Mom.

I did. Mom suggested a local caterer. I called him and explained my predicament. He agreed to lend me his facility before 9:00 a.m. and after 5:00 p.m. I had no idea how to use his equipment or how to shift from small batches made in my home oven to large batches made in an industrial oven.

I remember him. Big guy with a scary voice. Ever notice how most chefs are big?

You're off-topic. Two weeks of cooking, and I had the 80 kilos of granola needed for the event.

I helped. I was the same height as the mixer.

You did. You were fierce, Clo. Just 8 years old, and what a work ethic. The cool part is I did it all because of the memory of Linda, my mother's friend who'd died of breast cancer. No other motivation.

The morning of the event, I walked around the hotel ballroom, observing the attendees. Without realizing it, Sara had created a giant taste-testing for Grandma Emily's Granola. People were asking me where they could buy it. They couldn't. That was my aha moment.

It took me two weeks to screw up the courage but I finally called the hotel's executive chef, asking him if he had seen the product served that morning. "I saw it," he said. "I hated it. Come see me tomorrow morning at 6:00 a.m."

Clever man.

Clever is right. He didn't hate it. That was my first test. Imagine, a 6:00 a.m. meeting with three little kids at home. Another impossible logistic. It was my first foray into a commercial kitchen, armed with a half dozen small containers of granola, and the rest is history. He became my client and a great supporter.

That's how it started. Because Max ran in the door.

Because Grandma pushed me. Because Max ran in the door. Because I lost all financial support. Because of a hundred other moments of co-incidents that allowed me to fulfil the dream to support my three children. There were many sleepless nights, many long hours and long weeks, many suppers where all you kids had to eat was granola.

There was the intent, Mom. Intention is four-fifths of the way to completion. Because your intention was pure, the elements moved to accommodate you.

I had a really strong belief in the value of my product. I still do. All these years later, I still have it for breakfast almost every morning. No bank would grant any credit. I was too proud to ask any family members to co-sign, so I bootstrapped it.

Bootstrapping—13 letters. Those double letters are so sexy.

You're obsessed, Clo. I remember telling your dad I was going to make granola. "Why don't you go get a real job?" he said.

That was all I needed. If I hadn't felt sure about my decision before, I was now completely fired up.

Gotta get obsessed and stay obsessed.

I did. I was obsessed with this new entity called Grandma Emily's Granola. I worked every possible waking and sleeping moment.

Sleeping too. I like that. You know this business about sleeping when you're dead couldn't be further from the truth. It's almost non-stop growth and discovery.

You don't sleep, right?

Right. No sleeping, no eating. No bodily functions or grooming or any physical stuff. It's the realm of thought and vibration. I haven't actually crossed over yet, so I can only tell you how I am right now. I am here to fulfil this mandate with you.

So where are you?

Kind of in between states, so that we can communicate easily. Once I really cross over, this personality of Chloe melts back into the oversoul and will communicate with you occasionally, but not like we're doing now. It will be continuing on its own journey. Grandmother Emily did the same thing.

She did. I felt it too. Several years after starting the business, I had minor surgery that necessitated general anaesthetic. When I woke up after surgery, I could feel she was gone. I cried and cried. Only then did I feel the loss of her. I did ask her where she was going.

"I'm going to the Omega," she said. I had no idea what that meant at the time, but I have since learned that the beginning is the Alpha and the ending is the Omega. She's going right to the ultimate end. Go, Grandma, go.

We were talking about bootstrapping and the business, but I'd really like to speak of vibration because it is the key to having this communication in the first place. You know that every colour vibrates. You also know that you vibrate. Your heartbeat is a vibration that heads outwards each time it beats. So imagine then that these elements all interact—the colour you're wearing, the beat of your heart, the beat of others' hearts, the colour of your partner's shirt. Imagine how intricate this web is. Pick up the subtle vibrations of how colours feel, how you feel in someone's presence, how it feels to walk in a certain room.

John was just telling me yesterday how it happened perhaps 50 times in his career: a woman would walk in a house he was showing her, would get not even two feet inside and would tell him, "This is my house." Or, she would be in the entrance and immediately say, "Sorry, I can't even walk into this house. I have to leave."

Such is the power of vibration. We have the long view, Mom. We can see intent, motivation, strength, weakness, love and hate. If we choose to, we can see all truths from a life. We all can. All these states translate into vibratory colours and frequencies, and they can be seen from this perspective. That's why prayer is so potent and shines such a strong light outwards.

We walk beside you, we hold your hand, we caress your cheeks, we talk to you. We are with you. If our presence could be picked up more easily by humans, we'd be all banging into each other constantly. That's how present we are in your lives. All should know this. Do you know why I'm doing this?

Why?

I'm doin' it for the money!

You make me laugh. You really do.

Seriously, I'm doing this for the big payout, the gold medal, the multiple endorsements, the cover of Time Magazine.

Which, of course, begs the question: what is the big payout?

To fulfil my mission that offers a purpose for every suffering I endured.

I get it. I really do. The ripple effect of that is the fulfilment of my purpose in this mission too. Correct?

Correct. Today, you spoke to your friend Paul. The moment you met Paul decades ago, you felt a deep connection to him. You felt a love so strong that it confirmed what you always thought: that our relationships repeat, reconfigure and renew through our incarnations. They do.

This allows for more time spent in learning, growth and self-actualization, and less in trying to establish connections. They already exist from lives lived. This way you can efficiently pick up where you left off in your evolution. The introductions have long since been made.

Those *R*s. Nice going.

I think of the logistics needed to keep all these networks coherent and organized. Unfathomable.

Just think of the inner workings of the body, then multiply it by seven billion, and you have the intricacies of the real world wide web.

So we have the mandate to write this book together?

We do.

You are well-placed. We are a mother-daughter duo. You've been through enough to no longer doubt this material. You are less and less intimidated by the criticism of others. You've proven your love by sticking with me through the mess of my life. You loved me where I was. Life made you humble, tough, strong, compassionate, wise and generous. You're ready for this.

I am. At one point, I wanted to keep this conversation just between us. I love talking to you, Clo. It not only heals me, but it feeds me too. I can hear you. I know you're alive and well. I figured why set myself up for judgement and for the role of defending this material? Why not just enjoy this between us and get on with my life?

And the answer, ladies and gentlemen, is …

Well, you made it clear, in no uncertain terms, that we should continue. First, I had this ultra-frustrating dream. In the dream, I'm starting a race, but I have to change, I have to pee, I am constantly searching for something I can't find. The teams are ready. Daylight is fading. I'm getting lost in a maze. I can hear myself saying. "C'mon, AC, hurry up, you're stalling. You're dragging your butt. Get on with it!"

I wake up and realize it's a clear message to quit dragging my feet and getting sidetracked.

You gave me everything I need to complete this project. I absolutely wanted to live surrounded by beauty. Check. I needed the time and the financial independence to do this, so I got the revenue from selling the business last year after running it for almost two decades. Check. You knew I didn't want to and actually couldn't live without love, and you gave me John. Check. I also wanted to be nurtured by friends, and you've placed me just minutes away from my two dearest friends. Check.

Check, check, check. Looks like you got it, Mom. How did you like your evening last night?

My meditation evening was a powerhouse. Congratulations, Clo, you got your wings. I saw them: black. You're a black angel. I felt them completely surround and hug me. I heard you apologize for those times when you would deliberately not hug me. Those mornings when I wanted to give you a hug, but you withdrew and were aloof.

But you felt it totally last night. You also got my message of the book being the now project. Once it's done, I'll be on my way. The fears of criticism and judgement of others are roadblocks you are placing in your way. One more thing: wear white, Mom.

I got that while I was in the shower this morning.

Wear white to remind you and prompt you to surround yourself with the divine white light of love. Here are my last wishes.

I wish to drink a milkshake.

I wish to dance in the rain.

I wish to cuddle my baby brother.

I wish to blow out 75 candles on my cake.

I wish to learn how to tightrope walk.

I wish to ride a bike across the country.

I wish to eat peanut butter out of the jar.

I wish to kiss my mother, hold her and cry.

I wish to know cold and hot and in between.

I wish to lie in the grass and feel it tickle my neck.

I wish you to know that I live, I dance, I hug, I tickle and I am close to you.

Thanks, Clo. If a hug could be written, it would feel like this wish list, bookended by a milkshake and a tickle. Just noticed how the lines descend like the side of a pyramid. Very cool.

What's the story with retail therapy? You've been mentioning it to me all week.

I was obsessed to go out and shop. I wanted to be a part of a world that didn't want me in it. We went to the mall, but people stared. She looks like she's dying, *they thought.*

They were right. But even dying people want to wear a new scarf. Dying people are still living until they're dead. Its sounds like stating the obvious, but the meaning is subtle. Think about it: they still love music. They still can feel the breeze on their necks. They still love scarves. They still want to look beautiful.

I wanted to especially thank you for dressing up that day last summer.

Which day, Clo?

I'd been bugging you, harassing you to take me shopping. Again and again, I wanted to go shopping. Even if I bought something worth

50cents, I needed to buy something. You asked me why I wanted to shop. Do you remember now?

I remember because somehow you made the audio recording play itself while I was driving yesterday. That was really freaky, Clo. I just about jumped out of my skin while driving at 115 km per hour. I made over a hundred audio recordings while I was taking care of you. I have no idea which number that one was yesterday, but it was the one where I told the story of asking you why you wanted to shop, and what you answered. It was really touching.

It was easy to make it work because it takes an ultra-light touch to activate the recorder.

Hmm. That gives me an idea to explore another time: a Ouija board with a touch screen. Well, it really surprised me. I almost went off the road. I hadn't heard that recording since I'd made it. In fact, I haven't heard most of them. What amazes me is you knew exactly which one to press to tell me that retail therapy story.

You wanted to shop because you wanted to feel beautiful. That's when I realized how important it was to you to still feel you were in a body that was alive. So we both got all dressed up, with make-up and jewellery and the works, and went out.

That was one of the kindest things you did for me. You asked me what I wanted. That so validated me, loving me as I was. It was acceptance of me. You recognized what I needed, and you made it happen. Thank you.

Having trouble writing. Sometimes I get totally overwhelmed emotionally. As much as I know to stay calm in order to hear you properly, sometimes it just gets too tough, too raw. My heart hurts. Gotta get up and take a break before my heart breaks. I want cookies. I want chips. I can't stop eating. I'm gonna soak in a nice hot bath and do a facial. I'll be back.

Keep falling, keep falling, keep falling in love with life. Fall in love, spring in love, summer in love and finally winter in love with life.

This is some exercise. Not for the faint-hearted. Besides it being cathartic and a healing journey for me, we have a mandate to fulfil. You helped me see that the mandate is to show that this discussion is possible. It is not simply for the few with clairvoyant abilities, or for sages or highly evolved beings. It is available to all.

In the interests of how to communicate with loved ones who've passed, I'd like you to delineate some concrete actions that make the process possible.

Not everyone can sing opera. Not everyone can swim the English Channel. The truth is almost no one can do either of the above. Why then should people believe they can train themselves to speak across the divide?

Because if at least one person can do something, others can do it as well. Because the point is not to declare that this conversation can be commonplace; it is to bring awareness that it happens, that the divide can be bridged. Death is truly a renewal of life, a continuation of the journey. There is only life after life. Because everyone encounters death—100 percent of us die.

We have the visceral, intimate knowledge of grief associated with death. It is the second-most primal experience after the first cry associated with the first breath. It is the cry of no more breath. This is all that is needed to qualify for the role.

If people can allow for this possibility, they can reduce their fears, assuage their grief, and open themselves to this hopeful reality, whether or not they hear their loved ones.

Not everyone wants to sing opera, but if you have some talent and work hard enough, you can teach yourself to be an opera singer. Talking to spirit is the same thing.

Some people are born that way. Some aren't interested at all. Some, through a predisposition or through lifetimes of honing and working towards the goal, have the opening to spirit. What if people simply consciously choose to develop that capacity? Can they?

Absolutely.

Okay, so how can we help people go about preparing and then initiating this conversation?

Preparation is the key word. Let's call it the 12 Steps to Bridging. They aren't necessarily in the appropriate sequence, except for number one.

The 12 Steps to Bridging

1. All is as it should be

Fundamental to this initiative is the understanding that all is as it should be with the world. There will be much evidence to contradict that statement. Ignore it. This is the toughest step. It's called acceptance.

All is as it should be. This applies to all things in life and death. Not only are there no mistakes in life (just lessons), but there are no errors in death. Every life is appropriate and of the correct length. This fundamental knowing may be the subject of study during multiple lifetimes, or it may be known instantly. It requires the full acceptance of death as a part of life.

2. Stay calm, have patience and be aware

Wanting to connect, expecting to connect and heavy grieving will make the signal garbled and unclear. Have compassion for the phenomena of loss and continuous letting go, yet learn non-reactivity in order to maintain perspective and the practice of step number one.

Approach this like you're having a pedicure. You only have to choose your nail colour, close your eyes, follow the nudges to move your feet here and there and trust the work will be done. Stay aware.

3. Meditate every day

What that really means is cultivate silence. Silence outside and inside. Turn off the noise. Disconnect and allow yourself to be fed by the sound of your breath. Then listen.

4. Once you've disconnected, it's time to connect

Connect to the earth by grounding yourself. These types of communication require grounding, or else you'll wear yourself out. Then connect to yourself. One of the most powerful things you can do for yourself is to do nothing.

5. Write down what you get

Otherwise, like waking from a dream and expecting to remember it, the details will slip away if not recorded. You may see colours, hear a word or see an image. Record it.

6. Raise your vibration

Communicating across the veil involves the vibrational compatibility of both parties on either side. You have to raise your vibration to match the higher frequencies of more enlightened beings, and we who have passed have to lower ours.

The opposite is also true. Beings of a much lower order who carry disturbance, instability and illness can also latch on if your vibration is low enough. Therein lies enough impetus to keep raising your vibration.

On your end, you raise your vibration primarily through the food you eat. You also raise your vibration through sleeping properly, meditating and using mindfulness techniques. A group activity where two or more are gathered, such as attending a sound meditation circle and chanting, is often more effective than trying it solo. Experiment.

7. Create a ritual

Wear a certain piece of clothing or jewellery. Create ceremony, however small, to move from real life to awakened life.

8. Ask

First ask for protection. Then ask for clear evidence—something outside of your common knowledge to confirm the information is coming to you and not from you. Stay aware. Just like people are all shapes and sizes, so are our ways and means to reach you.

9. Believe and receive

Reverse the old adage "Seeing is believing." The correct phrase is "Believing is seeing." It will then become "Believing is receiving."

10. Share what you receive with others

To counteract the roadblocks the rational mind erects, commit to sharing the information received. When you share, it should resonate as authentic.

11. Give thanks for the communion

If you only realized how much we're all in, how much we're trying to assist, how much you resist yet we persist. You'd be thanking spirit a lot more often.

12. Be light about things

This is normal and natural. In less than two generations, it will be commonplace. Schools will teach energy work in their curriculums.

This is a two-way street. Initiating the communication has been mostly done from this side, although it can be initiated from the earth personality. Do not ask the entity to communicate too often; doing so is disruptive, and the communication may cease completely.

Interesting sidebar, Mom. You and I communicate on and off. It is not a constant conversation. That is the difference between you and a schizophrenic. A schizophrenic, like my brother Matthew, has a non-stop conversation with spirit. It never shuts off and is therefore a schizophrenic's constant, dominant reality.

A fine line indeed.

Also, Matt's low vibration attracts low-vibrating entities to him. It is an entirely different kind of communication designed to enslave, not empower.

From this side, we need to be very calm and use repeated focus in order to draw your attention to that exterior thought. Your attention may be continuously drawn to a particular object. A book can be recommended several times. Or perhaps a strange phrase repeats itself in your head until you acknowledge it. Be aware of the nudges. We also use electronics, which is making the communication much simpler since cell phones have become ubiquitous.

Once we cross all the way over, we are a lot less likely to contact you. This is for your good as well as ours. You need to grieve and then get over us. If we linger nearby, the relationship continues to dominate.

For me to remain close, like I'm doing now, requires me to feed off your energy. That's why this can be such an exhausting experience for you at times: your energy is my food. When I finally transition to the other side, I won't be as close by. You'll be able to move on, to think of me with love and tenderness but not be destroyed with grief.

I am here voluntarily. We both are, in fact. We've made this agreement to do this work together. Don't drag your feet.

What else can you tell me about where you are?

I'm in my consciousness. This is the Mothership, Mom. Earth is the satellite outpost, but this is home—for all of us. There are literally no dead-ends, only dead beginnings.

CHAPTER 10

No cul-de-sacs. No dead-ends. I like that, Clo. It sums up the experience of dying and how it's part of a soul's continuous journey.

I've just woken up from yet another nap. Lately, I'm always napping. I seem to be tired or recovering from being tired. A mind-numbing tiredness. Filling a glass of water and drinking it seems too daunting a task. It's the kind of tired where you feel like crying a lot.

It finally hit me that this is grief—deep, real grief. It lurked behind "I'm totally fine" and "She's happy and in a great place, and I'm happy for her." It completely reduced me to a lump on the floor that had split in two. I felt this break inside, and pain just oozed out. There were tears, but not many. Mostly it was real, physical pain. The release of sadness. I felt like my gut was pushed through a grinder. It lasted 10 minutes and then put me out for three days. I was bumping into stuff. But mostly I just stayed in bed, blindsided. All I felt like doing was eating and sleeping.

I noticed you just ate a whole bag of Tostitos.

I craved the salt. What else did you notice?

As weird as this sounds, I can notice just about everything. I noticed you stopped asking me stuff. You needed a break.

It came on just after I wrote down your 12 steps to bridging. It took me three days to write those down, and then my mind went numb, taking my body with it. I thought I had mono or some autoimmune issue. My good friend Sandra, who's worked extensively in palliative care, explained that this is healthy grieving. It's hitting me strongly because I can take it strongly. It doesn't mean I'm weak; it means I'm normal. According to Sandra, because we worked out most of our stuff while you were alive, this is grieving without regret or guilt.

It still felt like a massive punch to the stomach.

The centre of emotion.

Carole, my other amazing friend I consult for all things of spirit, told me I need to ground more. She explained that it's not normal to talk to spirit so much during a day.

You could incorporate a short prayer to protect you from energy overlapping. I coined that phrase. It means you give too much, and I take too much.

Sounds like our lives all over again.

It is our lives all over again. Just because I'm on this side doesn't mean that the same dynamics aren't prevalent.

A double negative!

Noted. Even on this side, the same relationship dynamics still present themselves from time to time. This will happen less as we readjust.

Just now, upon waking from yet another nap, I hear "black and white, black and white," repeating itself over and over.

Bravo. What I'm trying to tell you is that it is and it isn't black and white. You want this communication to be stark and clear—black and white. You want to be sure before you attribute something to me. That preoccupies you to no end.

It does.

Well, it has no end because it has no purpose. You ask me to tell you something incredibly outrageous. or to perform some kind of miracle so that everyone knows it's me and not you. Jesus had doubters even though he performed countless miracles.

Simply do the work and trust. You've survived lifetimes of communication with spirit. Accept the work and do it. I hear all your doubts; I hear your thoughts, Ma. I also know that you know beyond any doubt that this conversation is real. So practice acceptance, allowing and non-reactivity. Put the words down in black and white. Black and white. And let the universe do the rest. This will help you keep your energy in your heart, rather than dissipate it with endless thoughts in your head.

I can do this. I'd like to go through your 12 steps to bridging the divide and offer a personal narrative attached to each step.

Be my guest. Oh, no, Mom—we forgot entirely about the play.

Can't do everything, Clo. Gotta stay on topic. That will have to wait. If you stay close, once this book is done, maybe we could co-write the play?

Deal. Remember, I'm doin' it for the money.

You just love saying that, don't you?

I do.

Continue. Go. No more dooberhasimoniousness.

I just looked that up, and it's not a word.

Part of it is. Mom, a doober is a marijuana cigarette—a spliff, a joint. Dooberhasimoniousness refers to talking as if you're stoned, sleepy and stupid. It doesn't come close to Mary Poppins, but it works. I actually made it up: 21 letters.

A very cool construct. You're 13 letters short of Supercalifragilisticexpealidocious. That Sherman Brothers classic was added to the *Oxford Dictionary* in the 1980s, so there's hope for your crazy word, Clo.

A marijuana cigarette. You've got lots of experience with those. I remember the day you asked me to smoke with you. Here I am, thinking I'll be a cool Mom and smoke with my kid. One puff, and I felt so sick!

Then I watched you smoke the whole joint. A shiver went through my body, and I knew we were in trouble. That was long before you had smoked crack.

I knew I was living against my own values. I knew it was destroying me, but I couldn't stop it. It was too strong. How did we get here? I don't even like talking about this. I feel lousy, queasy.

So now you know how I felt for those three days I was out of it. You have no body, but you still feel?

We're energy, Mom. Emotion is energy in motion. I feel not only my own emotions but yours too, if I choose to tune in to them. That makes me think of something. When we press that reset button and cross over, and you guys are being all hysterical and crying and mourning for days and weeks, it really disturbs us. We are happy. We are free, home and complete. Please realize that all the grieving, while somewhat appropriate, is very upsetting for us. Can you try to be happy for us?

I don't actually mean you or Daniel, because you both get it and were happy for me.

We were, Clo. This is an old paradigm that is deeply entrenched as something terrible, woeful and demanding of displays of grief.

So much depends on the circumstances surrounding the death. A long, slow suffering like you experienced is processed differently than a sudden, tragic death. Death of a child is processed differently than the death of an elderly loved one.

We've set up all kinds of rules we adhere to that make some deaths manageable and others unacceptable. We don't consider it appropriate to celebrate a funeral; other cultures do. I wanted to throw you a party. Imagine how that would have gone off!

Ma, you've gotta love them as they are, egos and all. Some are ready; some never will be. Why do we get so off topic? Back to our regular scheduled programming—your reaction to the 12 days of Christmas.

My take on the 12 Steps of Bridging. Here goes.

The 12 Steps to Bridging

1. All is as it should be

Step one is huge. It is the fundamental mindset that death is a normal continuation of life. Yes, we grieve, and that is normal too. But there are no mistakes. Even the death of a child is as it should be. For a parent, this is almost an impossibility to accept.

You said there is no such thing as a sudden death; all deaths are planned. This is beyond my comprehension. I realize that many things—most things—are beyond my comprehension.

The near-death experience I had in 1991 showed me that there is so much more going on than I realize. It illustrated the rule of time as not being linear. How was I able, at 7:00 a.m., to see the events that would happen that coming evening at 10:00 p.m.?

It taught me that we are loved, protected and never alone. It gave me courage and hope and opened my heart to all the lessons that followed. I realize how valuable that event was in teaching me that all is as it should be. It gave me the courage to offer this conversation to others. Every connected dot has brought me to this here and now.

I do accept that the universe is a perfect design of thought manifested into three dimensions and beyond. Manage your thoughts, and you manage to create the world you want to live in. What is, is what we've created. Want to create differently? Think different thoughts.

This is how I managed to cope with all the heartaches of your life, Clo. Even when I was searching for you on the streets, looking behind garbage containers and in dirty alleyways, I would tell myself to breathe, pray and trust.

The last year of your life was filled with so much heartache, little things and big things. Seeing you go to bed at 7:30 p.m. on a beautiful summer evening. Wishing instead that you were going out with friends. Watching your body deteriorate. I remember once you told me, "Mom, my body is starving me to death." Seeing the tumour protruding out of your abdomen, your struggle to walk and maintain your balance. The constant throwing up.

How your lovely fingers became so listless on top of the sheets. That last facial. The bump on your nose. Those long eyelashes and deep, searching, dark eyes. It was hard to accept that things were as they should be. I so wanted them to be different.

When a loved one suffers, acceptance seems an impossibility. It seems insensitive, cold and unfeeling. To use your words, Clo, it is a process fraught with roadblocks.

"All is as it should be." I repeat this often. Gradually grief diminishes, and acceptance takes over. Knowing that death is a return to love helps.

Step one is so much more than accepting death. It is the central belief that shifts us from being victims of the deeds of others to being students of life. Accepting that all is as it should be means accepting responsibility for all actions, all deeds. It means taking the view from 10,000 feet that any act perpetrated on my brother is perpetrated on me too. If someone suffers, I suffer. We are one massive, connected unit. Also, if my brother commits an act of aggression, I am responsible for that too.

"All is as it should be." These seemingly simple six words tell us that we live in the world of our creation. Way before I was truly able to embrace acceptance in my heart, I was trying to understand it cerebrally. You in one hospital. Matthew in another. I struggled. Then acceptance became a knowing. I have no idea when the switch happened; it simply did.

2. Stay calm, have patience, be aware

Mundane acts requiring no mental activity put me in that daydream state, where my thoughts are quiet but my mind is still alert.

I love the pedicure analogy. Choose and then sit back, relax and close your eyes—but don't fall asleep. You still have to stay aware enough to move your feet in the water, out of the water, on the towel, off the towel.

It's like placing your car keys deliberately in one place so that you always know where to retrieve them, versus plunking them down absent-mindedly when you get home. Deliberately remarking that the coffee pot has been turned off frees the mind of "Did I remember to turn off the coffee?" A certain deliberate awareness frees the mind and keeps me on my toes.

There are so many ways for you to signal you're nearby. One of my favourites is smell. It is so distinct, and there's no mistaking that odour when it hits. There's also no mistaking its link to you. We have to be sensitive to the possibilities, open to the signals around us that can be so subtle. We won't even stand a chance if we're fretting, stressed or preoccupied.

3. Meditate every day

This was tough when I was a single working mother. Tough, but not impossible. Cultivating silence, on the other hand, was always possible. Meal preparation and driving were moments when silence could reign. I simply turned off the radio, the phone, the TV.

Even today, with time to spare, meditating every day takes a certain discipline that escapes me sometimes. I know meditation brings clarity of mind, and clarity of mind brings space to hear guidance.

4. Disconnect and then connect

Connecting to spirit has been a lifelong endeavour. My biggest frustration has not been knowing whether I'm being guided; it's been finding ways to listen properly. If only I could listen more. If only I could hear more clearly.

How to find the time while scrambling with the demands of life? When I was younger, I did hear the guidance, and then I'd often do the opposite. Instead of the high road, I would choose the fun road or the easy road or the adventurous road. Self-sabotage kept me on the wrong road.

Until this happened. It was a lovely, perfect day on Mexico's west coast. The sea was calm, and the sun was high. I decided to swim out to a coral reef about a hundred feet out. I was alone except for the attendant languishing on the water's edge by the snorkel hut.

It was a blissfully perfect day for a swim. As my toes touched the water, I heard a voice tell me in no uncertain terms, "Andrea, don't go in the water today. Do not go in. Danger."

I heard it. It made no sense, and I reasoned it away. I put on the flippers and a snorkel mask, and in I went. Minutes later, I look down, and there's a nine foot grey shark swimming directly under me. All I could see was a huge, toothy grin. Terrified but trying not to broadcast it, I turned slowly back towards shore.

While moving ever so slowly to not attract attention, I shifted my gaze towards the shore and began repeating a prayer my Grandmother Emily had given me. "If you are with Him and in His constant care, no harm will ever touch you, God's love is always there." I made it to shore, told the attendant what I'd seen and didn't go near the water again for the rest of the trip. Days later, there were reports of someone being seriously wounded by a shark attack in that area.

If this kind of guidance was available, why wasn't I listening fully? I decided it was time to start.

I began to meditate, and sometimes it was just five minutes a day. It was five consistent minutes, and it made a difference. I began to hear the guidance more clearly. Five minutes gradually became 20.

5. Writing down what I receive

Between 2010 and 2012, I received much information through inspired writing sessions. These sessions were magical. I would sit with a pen and paper and start writing. The material came out fully formed and without error. It was effortless.

This work with you is different. I write, I ask and I listen for a response. Sometimes you're right there. Sometimes you're not, so I garden, cook, go for a walk, exercise or do laundry. When I do hear you, I drop what I'm doing and head for the computer. I need to record your words when they present themselves, even if it's at 4:00 a.m. *Especially* if it's at 4:00 a.m.

Inspiration comes and goes. I've learned to keep a notebook with me. A cell phone with voice recorder also works well.

6. Raising my vibration

Attending an evening of sound healing every week has had a huge positive impact on raising my vibration. Carole, a five-foot blonde with curls that surround her face like a halo, uses various crystal bowls to fill the room with vibration. They have the power to vibrate right through me.

Carole's crystal bowls

I feel my insides melt into sound, oscillating from the right side of my body to left and back again. I'm completely engulfed in the phenomenon of powerful pure vibration. The sound is so vast, so massive, that there's no room for anything else. One experiences pure nothingness. The effect is profound and lasts for days. Carole also uses other music to complement the experience. It has become like food for me.

I understand that the physical body, by its very nature, is heavy. It vibrates at much lower frequencies than beings with no bodies to lug around. In order for us to connect, we must go up enough to be able to be around your vibration. And you generously come down to meet us. Eating food with a high vibration is critical. Better food means a clearer mind. Above-ground food that has been kissed by the sun is my favourite.

7. Create a ritual

I used to do a small ritual around a lovely red ring that my mother gave me. It was my writing ring. One day, the stone fell out, and I just kept writing. That was the end of that ritual.

If I find I'm wandering and wasting time, a ritual does help centre me into the process, but I admit I'm not very disciplined about this one. Sometimes I simply light a candle. I like your distinction between real life and awakened life. I am not always consistent with saying a ritual for protection even though I know this is essential. A favourite prayer is this one.

> May the divine white light of love fill up this room
> and fill each one of us. For we are here, in love,
> with love, for the love of God and all our fellow

> human beings. We ask our guides from the spirit world to please come forth and guide us. Help us to be aware of who we really are: beings of light, beings of love. Protect us in this communication as well as in our daily lives, and help us to be one with the divine white light of love. So we thank you for being here for us and we love you. Amen.

As I speak these words, a strong coat of protection wrap itself around me.

8. Ask, ask, ask

I'm always being reminded to ask. We need to initiate communication and ask for guidance. The biggest stumbling block I have to asking is thinking I'm unworthy of being heard by spirit. That's my own self playing small. I've learned to get over that after being repeatedly told I'm worthy. I matter. We all matter.

We ask, and then we allow the answer to be given back to us.

Those strange words you tell me, Clo, which I've never heard before and don't know the meaning of, are tangible proof that what I'm hearing is from you not me.

9. Believe and then receive

It may seem difficult to blindly believe in something we have no concrete proof of, but we certainly have many near-death accounts too numerous and similar to be fraudulent. We have the work of mediums such as John Edward, Suzanne Giesemann, Rosemary Altea and others. We also have our own experience of feeling loved ones who've crossed over being close to us, communicating with us. This is not new.

I've been through enough to no longer worry about criticism from sceptics. I think I'm the biggest sceptic I know.

10. Sharing with others

The world needs to know that stepping out of the physical body is simply a soul continuing its journey. Knowing you are happy, well-surrounded, loved and continuing your growth means everything to me. It brings me peace and hope and great comfort. For these reasons, I want to share what I've experienced with others.

11. Gratitude

One of my favourite gratitude exercises is to say, "Thank you, Lord," as I walk or drive down a street. I simply gaze at something, even if it's a sign for a crosswalk, and say thanks. This exercise fills me with the gratitude vibe and bathes every cell in that essence. Thank you for not giving up on me.

12. Don't take myself too seriously

Life is good. It's hard to find the fun in something like suffering and death, but we can find the lessons. We can see beyond the immediate pain to appreciate the bigger picture. In doing this, we can lighten up a bit and try to bring the melodrama down a notch.

I know this life is but a blink in my existence. What seems so difficult, so traumatic, will morph into a classroom when I change my viewpoint. Being a witness helps me take myself less seriously. It allows me to mess up, to feel lazy, to act petty, to get confused and then to climb out of all that one baby step at a time.

Well done. Supercalifragilisticexpealidocious!

CHAPTER 11

I want to hear more! But first, I have an exercise for you: counting acts of love. I call them AOLs.

If you observe, they serve continuously. Just take this morning and start counting.

I like that, Clo. Counting acts of love. First, there were the ducks, showing up right at my doorstep.

AOL 1—The male and female duck couple that are inseparable. They show up here almost every day. They come to be fed, to snooze in the grass and to hang out on the stone wall. I care about them now. I worry for their welfare. For a couple of days, I didn't see the female. John and I went looking for her. He finally found her in the bushes.

They trust me. I sing to them and feed them. The female is less timid than the male. She now approaches within 16 inches of me. He's still a bit skittish, staying about four feet away.

AOL 2—John arrives with a hot coffee for me.

AOL 3 & 4—I make a strawberry rhubarb compote with the maple syrup given to me by my wonderful cousin Anita, using the fresh rhubarb from our garden.

AOL 5—John and I sit together, eat breakfast and chat. Then off he goes to an appointment.

AOL 6—I decide to do laundry, and because his stuff is in the dryer, I fold it all for him.

AOL 7—Time to meditate now, an AOL for myself.

All these AOLs, and it's only 9:00 a.m. It's amazing what you can find when you look for it. Thanks, Clo. Counting AOLs is my new math. I feel showered, blessed.

They're everywhere. Recognize them. Our job, our obligation, is to look for those acts of love. Unpack and appreciate them in all their forms.

They are everywhere, being offered up by everyone.

Wherever we are, they are too.

My days and nights were filled with acts of love to you, Clo. Mostly you didn't bother to acknowledge them, almost never saying thanks. To me, that was the worst prison of your own doing: the prison of being cut off from gratitude. Your world was a stark place.

I can feel you crying now. Does that mean you still shed tears?

I shed emotion. Nothing can be hidden so if I feel it, it communicates. Instantly and powerfully.

None of your thoughts are hidden either. People, are you listening? There are no secrets.

We operate as if our thoughts are our own secret domains. It's time to get control of our minds, isn't it?

Oui, Maman.

I'm beginning to understand how you functioned. To acknowledge the kindness of others is to know you're worthy of receiving such kindness. I believe this was the big issue with you. Better to not acknowledge the acts of kindness. Better to believe you're unlovable and irreconcilable. It is not true, of course.

So, AOLs matter, big and small. Preparing you a meal, straightening out a blanket, putting a cold cloth on your forehead, giving you a massage, a manicure, cleaning your room … on and on these acts define us as human, as caring and loving actors. Acts of love.

This is common knowledge but bears repeating. When we push the reset button, we take with us all the love we've received. We take the love. Every act of kindness, every act of love is with me. My illness was an opportunity to love. That's pretty much what it was, Mom. I was so bitchy. I tried to make it hard for you. I did make it hard for you and everyone else, but you still loved. And so I transcended that sicko body, and your love made me whole.

Why is it that love makes us whole?

Because love is really all there is. All else are roadblocks we set up so that we have to fight our way back to love. Fear is a roadblock. Judgement of others and the self is a roadblock. Self-doubt is a huge roadblock. Only love is real. That's why we make love. We can actually make love. By acts of love, we make love grow. That growing connects us to others, to the universe, and makes us whole.

The words capture only a small part of the concept you're describing. It's as if one has to simply experience this to know it. There is no homework to do or lessons to learn. There is simply an AOL to acknowledge. Acknowledging the act of love leads us towards more love.

Even my words aren't adequate. Maybe I'll tell you a story, and this can describe what I mean. I'd like to tell you about Maurice.

I met Maurice the first day you were admitted to the hospital palliative ward. He was in his late 60s and had malignant tumours throughout his body. Some were visible on his legs. One was enormous, the size of a football. It seemed horrific at first, but his kind, gentle smile led me back to seeing him as a human being, not a science experiment.

Maurice spent so much time shuffling down those halls that we saw him often during the month we spent there. We'd chat a little, exchange a smile and sometimes engage in a real conversation. He knew he was dying. He spoke frankly about welcoming death and about the blessed nature of life. What struck me about Maurice was the clarity of his mind. I had always equated dying with old age and senility, but the palliative ward taught me otherwise.

On the night you died, after I had spent almost two hours with your body, the orderly came in to prepare you for the morgue. I was still trying to process you going from a burning fever the night before to being stone cold. Your eyes were open, but no light shone.

When we spend time with the body of a loved one, it becomes clear that we are spirits housed in temporary shells.

I truly think the mind has an off switch that creates a numbness in the emotions, a going through mechanical motion without emotion. This overload switch gets tripped perhaps only a handful of times in a life, when the energy surge risks overwhelming the circuits. This was one such moment. Knowing I would never see you again. Knowing this was my last chance to memorize those freckles, to caress your hair, to touch your face.

I couldn't watch the orderly do his work. Was there was a soundproof room where I could howl in pain? The attending physician shook his head. No such room existed. It should.

To get hysterical would have made things worse for you and

for all those sleeping in that ward. Maintaining self-control made things tougher for me. It was brutal but essential.

An adjacent ward of the hospital was vacant. I went there to walk the empty corridors. The eeriness of those vacant halls: they had once teemed with life; now they were the perfect setting for the numbness that enveloped me. Grief washed itself upon me in varying doses. Along with grief was relief that you were free.

I wanted to crawl into a small closet and hide. I wanted a hug. It was 4:30 a.m. I wanted to howl. I wanted to be silent so that I could feel your presence. I wanted to feel a human touch. And then I saw Maurice, calmly shuffling down those empty halls.

He smiled sweetly, asking me how you were. I told him you had just passed. We hugged, linked arms and silently walked those deserted halls together, the only sound the shuffle of Maurice's slippered feet. Whatever mess of emotion I was in, the comfort Maurice offered was just right, just enough to get me over the hurdle of those few hours.

Maurice passed about a month after you. Thank you, Maurice, for that act of love when I most needed it. His last days served to comfort me. What greater purpose can a life have than to be of service to another?

I remember the sound of his slippers down the hallway. That's some heavy writing. "Open-heart surgery without anaesthetic" writing.

CHAPTER 12

Mom, I want to hear more about your business. Also, you had started to tell me about when you were first on your own with three kids, no job and no money. What did you do? How did you get out of it?

At first, I wasted a bunch of brain cells hoping that some Prince Charming would rescue me and my brood from the burning castle. That didn't happen. What did happen is that all three of you got the chicken pox. For two weeks, it was round-the-clock baking soda baths and misery all around. It was like a purging of something, and that purge was literally happening through everyone's skin. We were all shedding something.

I remember walking in the woods near our home. It was the only place we could go with all those marks on all of you. Matthew was 6, you were 4 and Daniel was 2. An old man in the woods looked at me and asked, "Are those your kids?"

"Yes," I said, feeling desperately sad, lonely and overwhelmed.

"You must be so proud of them," he said.

I managed a wan smile. *Proud?* I thought. *Proud? I'm feeling too exhausted to cook a meatball. That's what I'm feeling.* All I could imagine was an abyss of frenzied single parenthood sucking me dry. I was exhausted.

Besides the meatballs, Mom, what actually happened? How did you do it? How did you go from broke with three kids and a big ego that wouldn't allow you to ask for help to an independent, successful entrepreneur?

Wish I could tell you a magic plug-and-play formula. It was simply single-minded focus. And no debt. None. If I could afford it, I bought it; otherwise, I went without. It wasn't how much I earned that counted. It was how little I spent.

I sold my car. Imagine, starting a business with three young kids and no car. The proceeds from selling my Honda kept me going for a few months.

If I was to write a book about my experiences, it would be entitled *No Plan B*. That was my all-in approach. An idea, a strong why, very little money, no credit and a grandmother who believed I could do it.

I only remember you worked a lot, day and night. How did you know what you were doing?

I didn't. I had great teachers. Mostly money was my biggest teacher. Lose a little money, learn a little lesson. Lose a lot of money, learn a big lesson.

For example, I needed a lawyer to incorporate my company. I didn't want to simply register a name. I wanted to have a federally incorporated entity so I could sell all over the country. The fee was about $600. Then there were fees for trademarking the name and other essential paperwork. I needed about $1,600 in all.

I packed a large suitcase full of ladies leggings and T-shirts, mostly slightly irregular pieces from your dad's factory, and headed downtown to a large office building. I arrived just in time for the lunch hour, as the women were exiting the elevators and heading towards the food court. And right there, I sold my wares. I also had small sample sizes of granola for people to taste. Feedback was encouraged, and their comments were encouraging.

It was an act of humility to put myself out there so publicly. I told myself that if I had the guts to do that, I could do anything. In just two days, I sold everything and raised the money I needed to take the next step: incorporate a company and trademark the name Grandma Emily's Granola.

I asked a trusted accountant which lawyer he would recommend to file the necessary paperwork. He gave me a name. I made the contact and paid the money up front.

Then nothing. No news, couldn't reach him. A highly recommended individual who was nowhere to be found. I called the trademark office. No money had been paid. The work had not been completed. The lawyer had skipped town. The first of many lessons learned.

That's rough, Mom. You sold leggings downtown at lunchtime?

Yup.

And then the crooked lawyer took the cash?

Yup.

You told no one how you started with no money?

No one.

I'm not sure if you were crazy, brave or just plain desperate.

Maybe all of the above. I had three kids to take care of. Maybe your father thought I'd go running to my family to bail me out. I couldn't do that. I didn't want anyone's pity. So it was one day at a time. The material world became immaterial as I focused on the essentials: raising my kids and a business at the same time.

Today, there's a name for that. It's called bootstrapping, and it's now considered a legitimate business model. I'm one of the people championing that strategy.

I had no money and lacked a lot of the necessary skills. I knew nothing about running a food business, about hiring and firing, about anything. I knew my three kids needed a roof and needed to eat.

Keeping the books was complicated for me. Cold-calling was humbling. Hiding my desperation was surprisingly easy. I loved driving a bargain with suppliers and was completely dedicated to making this idea work. I learned another big lesson soon after starting in business. Want to hear it?

Does it involve losing more money?

Yup. Way more.

Ah. I dunno if I want to hear it. This is getting painful.

No worries, Clo. Everything turns out okay in the end. Okay?

Okay, tell me.

I was just starting out. I wanted to sell my granola in retail grocery stores and neighbourhood small stores, so I approached a store and asked them who was a distributor they really liked to deal with.

I figured I couldn't make the granola, sell the granola, and do all the shipping too. The shipping part would take all my time. Plus, I had you guys to take care of. This one store recommended a distributor who handled similar products. I met him, and we worked out a deal. Now I could focus on manufacturing, and he could sell and ship. Right?

Right.

Wrong. He placed a first order for about $5,000 and paid me a week later. Encouraged by this, I granted him 30-day terms. He placed a second order. When that invoice was paid within the 30-day period, I figured I could trust him. Wrong again.

After I had extended him credit for roughly $15,000, he calls me on a Friday afternoon to tell me, "Sorry, Andrea, I won't be able to pay you your receivable in full. Here's a cheque for $5,000. That's it."

"What? What do you mean, that's it? Let's figure out a payment schedule. Let's look at some other arrangement, let's talk."

He didn't want to talk. The following Monday morning, he was found hanging in his office. He had killed himself.

One skips town, and one skips out of his life. What a rough start for you. How awful for everyone.

I remember going to his funeral, and his wife was so angry at him. He'd killed himself just days before his daughter was set to graduate from high school. He'd thrown a hand grenade into many people's lives. Rather than express compassion, everyone was pissed at him for something. I tried to keep reminding myself that he did give me a cheque for $5,000 to soften the blow. I had to take a $10,000 bad debt. I wanted to give up.

It was my constant preoccupation to not forget an appointment or a home-and-school meeting, to pick up supplies for a classroom art project, to do laundry, to pay the bills. Baseball, swimming, school outings, groceries, cooking—on and on.

One night, as I collapsed as usual in bed, the phone rang. It was 9:15 p.m.

Maria asked oh so politely, "Andrea, are you coming soon to get Chloe?"

Oh, my God—my deepest fear was realized. That was 20 years ago, and I remember it like yesterday.

You forgot me at Maria's house?

I'm not proud of that one.

A thousand baby steps later, things began to improve. It took five years for me to stop questioning my decision to start my own business. With every purchase of equipment, every spoon and stainless steel table financed by my own cash flow, there were ongoing compromises that kept things small.

I am no business whiz, Clo. I just had a good why. I didn't create a huge company that employed hundreds. The most employees we had were 20. We did do something special. Step by step, a small team worked and improved and created something to be proud of. People used to ask how many employees I had. I used to answer, "How many employees does Lehman Brothers have?" The answer is none. They used to have 25,000. Sometimes people got it. Sometimes they didn't.

Twice I borrowed from my brother: once to buy equipment, and another time to do leasehold improvements to a new location. Both times I paid him back. Had I asked him or any other family or friend for more assistance, I know they would have helped. I didn't ask. I had screwed up my life with my own poor choices, so I kept my mess to myself. A mortgage was enough debt, thank you.

Grandma was always nearby, nudging me on, applauding my victories and chastising me when I made mistakes. She especially loved to go on sales calls with me. I could feel her standing right beside me, avidly listening. She would applaud a great call and criticize a bad one, offering ideas to improve my delivery and timing for the subsequent potential customer. She used to say, "Andrea, don't you dare screw up. That's my face you have on all those labels."

On Friday afternoons, after all the staff had left for the weekend, I would walk around the plant, talking to her and thanking her for supporting me. Without Grandma's inspiration, GEG would not have happened.

One day, Grandma declared that I wouldn't be running this company all my life. She told me I had bigger things to do and that the purpose of GEG, besides providing for my children, was to give me credibility. "GEG is a stepping stone," she said. "By creating something out of absolutely nothing, you'll have the credibility you need to go even further with your life's mission."

I was baffled and no closer to understanding what that mission was, but I trusted her completely and soldiered on. Now, all these years later, it is beginning to come into view.

These 10 easy steps to success came to me as I slept last night. Here they are.

Ten Easy Steps to Success

Step One: What am I going to do with my life?

Step Two: I have no idea.

Step Three: How much does it cost to raise three children?

Step Four: Faint.

Step Five: I don't know much, but I know how to make great granola.

Step Six: Ex-husband scoffs. "Why don't you go get a real job?"

Step Seven: Now I'm really stoked.

Step Eight: I jump in.

Step Nine: Giving up is not an option.

Step Ten: Eighteen years of honest, hard work. Sell.

In other words, there is no quick fix.

Exactly. I built GEG one client at a time, one spoon at a time. I was all about "small is beautiful." In fact, that phrase would shout itself out in my brain so often that one day, I decided to google it, and voila. I was introduced to E. F. Schumacher and his book, *Small Is Beautiful: The Study of Economics as if People Mattered.* It became a guide book of sorts, and it helped shape my view of the interdependence of everything on the planet.

I'm always amazed how everything I need to know, every answer I seek, always reveals itself when I'm in nature. I just walked my six kilometres on the lovely path I've been walking for years. This past April, while the ground was still snow-covered, I had ventured out for a walk in my running shoes. It was a bit of a tough go. I found myself using my arms more, pumping them to help me move through the snow.

Aha! That is how obstacles serve us in life. They help us to engage other parts of the self that may be dormant. We call upon our bigger, greater selves to move through obstacles that are throwing resistance in our way. Such is the value of the tough times. Such is the value of running shoes in the snow.

I'm thinking about freedom and what it truly means to me. Freedom from suffering? Freedom from loss? Not possible. Life manufactures suffering and loss. It's freedom from carrying the burden of those things. Freedom from maintaining the burdens of past sufferings and losses.

This matters because new suffering and losses are always

coming our way. Are we going to add to a growing pile, or are we going to move through them, grasp the lesson and let go?

So, how to do it? How to really unburden?

To me, the key is to not create the burden. If I've created the burden, the memory or the trauma, then I have to go back to it. That's just about the only way to heal it. I go back to that 6-year-old child that's inside me and give her what she needs to heal. Usually, it's an ear, a moment in my conscious mind and of course love.

Another thing I learned is to not make my choices wrong. If I did something that I later realize isn't in my highest and best interest, I need to realize that I thought it was at the time I made the choice; I was making that choice using the tools I had at the time. Making it wrong makes me wrong, makes me dishonour myself. So there are no wrong choices, just choices that lead to other choices.

I think of all the arguing when couples divorce, and I wonder if we could soften it a bit by remembering that we did once love each other. We did deliberately choose each other. When couples split, could they not deliberate more? We need to do more deliberation to bring about liberation.

Get this paradox. The word *deliberate* means to discuss and examine from different viewpoints. It also means to un-liberate, to de-liberate. To discuss something, to keep hashing it over and over, is to render us not free from it. The more we deliberate a topic, the more we invest in it emotionally and the more we compromise our own liberation. C'est bon, no? So this word is in itself an oxymoron, because to deliberate is to discuss and understand, yet it also means to impede liberation.

Word games—I love them.

I know. You are your mother's daughter.

CHAPTER 13

The Land of the Living versus the Land of the Dying

We can't be in both places at the same time. The energy is completely different. Caring for a dying child is being in the land of the dying. Shave the head, refuse every invitation and be present to the process.

Time used to rush by. A working mother struggling in a whirlwind of responsibility—school projects, lunches to make, laundry to fold, receivables to collect. Now, time is slow. Minutes creep by. The day does not move.

My Diary: February 5, 2016

My cousin Anita sends me a link to Chilly Gonzalez and his four-minute video about deconstructing music using Lana del Rey's version of "Don't Let Me Be Misunderstood." Gonzalez talks of the infinite loop of sadness, the optimism of the major chord, the advertising moment when the band stops and the name of the song comes through loud and clear—a great technique used over and over.

The infinite loop of sadness. Sounds like our lives, lived over and over: birth, death, birth, death. An infinite loop subject to the whimsy of a left instead of a right turn, a kiss or no kiss, a slip on wet rocks or a quick hand that reaches out to grab us. A crapshoot.

My Diary: February 7, 2016

Took a long time to massage her feet and hands today. The hands were so limp in my fingers. Gone, the tension and the fight in them. They were soft, soft hands that no longer toiled at anything. Funny how there's hardness where there's fight and resistance. Her tumour, large as a soup bowl and hard as a rock, takes over more and more of her abdomen. It's hard to imagine she is able to eat.

She asks me to massage her belly. I say yes. I have done it a few times now. The skin is stretched to a point where the contact place with the highest point of the tumour is completely red and irritated, and the skin is split. Like the thing wants to bust loose.

After I've been there about six hours, she tells me she needs alone time. I do too, actually. Being there is exhausting. She's so antsy that she can't stay in her bed.

At one point, she looks at me and asks, "Is this about the size of a one and a half?"

She's still imagining getting her own place. She's actually in a small hospital room, maybe 8 by 12 feet.

Jerry, a psychiatric patient who has lived in the hospital for years, comes to visit. He's kind of repulsive looking. Long grey beard with food stuck all over it. Dishevelled. Fingernails long and gross with fungus on them. He has trouble walking, talks out loud to himself and slurs his words. He seems to be overmedicated.

He's Chloe's friend. He brings her things. He visits almost every day. When he leaves, she tells him she loves him. Chloe gave him two packs of cigarettes a few days ago. He lost one. She gives him cigarettes all the time. I've never seen anyone visit Jerry, but that doesn't mean he has no family. It simply means they don't know how to handle him and his oddness.

The first day he shuffled over with his walker to Chloe's room, the nurse was alarmed and was going to call security.

"It's okay," I said. "It's Jerry. Chloe knows him." It's more than that. He is her friend. She hasn't many of those.

One day he's standing at the elevator, cursing an imaginary adversary. He's criticizing and angry. "Go easy, Jerry," I say. "Life's good."

He looks at me and agrees. "Maybe I was a bit too critical," he says in a normal voice. He calms down.

I meet Cyndi in the palliative ward. Her father has slept in the room beside her mother every night since arriving in palliative care. Oh, that a man who would love me that much.

All the other palliative patients—except for Maurice, who walks the halls constantly—are pretty much stuck to their beds, immobile. Not Chloe. Every half hour, she's up. Downstairs to smoke, then back upstairs. She's all over the hospital. Everyone stares as she rolls by. Today, with her cane, she actually walked all over. She even went by herself to smoke outside. Once outside, she crouches. It isn't easy to crouch like that. I tried it—ouch.

Crouch and ouch are close cousins. Like death personified, walking around the hospital reminding people of what is coming. Eyes widen as she passes by.

There is no keeping a vigil with Chloe. Because she's up all night and all day, snatching bits of sleep when she is finally overwhelmed by medication and fatigue, one can't stay in her room. I tried it for three nights. Three infernal, never-ending nights. She was up four or five times during the night, heading downstairs to smoke.

I was exhausted.

Note to Palliative Care Volunteers

Don't ask me where the cancer is. That becomes all about curiosity and meddling, and it's inappropriate. Ask about the patient. We all need to speak of the one we love. We need to recount stories, to keep their spunk and spirit vivid to ourselves and others, to show others what that person really looked like, really acted like. This person lying in the bed is not the person we knew, cared for, loved and still love. It is a stripped-down version that doesn't represent the majority of her years on earth. And we want others to know about those years, those victories. So ask us about them: what they were like, a really fond memory that stays with us and that personifies them or our relationship to them.

Even if I know there is no death and the spirit moves back into its more natural state before it carries on its growth and journey, there is still a finality to death in that it's the death of the physical. This becomes overwhelming if we've placed a lot of importance on the physical. And even if we haven't, and we recognize and celebrate their stepping out of the body, it still grieves us. We need private spaces to grieve, places where we can cry without being disturbed.

It's okay to smile. When you're happy, you help me shake off those old paradigms of "death equals morose and heavy sadness, whereas fun equals guilt." I still want to smile, be happy and have a sense of humour. We can do that together. We can buck the old ways of thinking about death so that we all can feel less guilty about still embracing life through this letting go process.

We can laugh a bit. We can smile. We can joke. Nothing repairs like a good ol' belly laugh.

Note to Others

Dialogue really helps. Talking about our shared symptoms, waking up with a start in the middle of the night, feeling exhausted with the long process, the meanness and sharp tongue of the sick family member, weariness over hospital food, noisy corridors, noisy elevators—whatever the issue, it helps to talk with someone who also lives it. The dialogue with other families is therapeutic.

This happens organically as we start seeing each other every day, day in and day out. Eventually we introduce ourselves, talk about who we're here with and then start chatting. It helps a lot. Yesterday, I mentioned to Cyndi how I was sad to see my son Daniel head back out west. Eyes tear up quickly, and she offers a hug. A total stranger offers a hug. I accept.

I think about the patients lying in palliative care right now. Are there things they want to say? Burdens they want to lift?

At 28, Chloe is by far the youngest kid on the block. Next in line is Cyndi's 67-year-old mother.

Some days are no-mascara days. Yesterday was one of those, and I couldn't stop crying. I gave her a hand massage. They were so fragile. I cried as I gave her a foot massage. Her toenails so hard. This is standard, apparently. As a person approaches death, the fingernails and toenails become brittle. I had trouble cutting them and cried again.

I stopped at H&M to pick up a top—a little retail therapy to change my mood. While punching in my PIN, I told the cashier, a total stranger, how sick Chloe is and how my heart is breaking. Poor her. Sharing grief is like unloading through the weep hole of life. She won't forget that sale anytime soon.

Sometimes there are no words. You've just gotta swim in it and swim out the other side.

I awoke in the middle of the night last night and saw a huge daisy. It took up all my vision, a giant daisy in my mind's eye. Then I began to sing, "Daisy, daisy, give me your answer do." The bicycle built for two is us, Clo. It's captured in that picture and will forever be remembered as one of the last things we did together.

I also dreamt I was trying to fit my feet into someone else's shoes, but their shoes didn't fit quite right. After trying and trying, I finally dipped my hand into the bag slung across my shoulder to find, much to my surprise, that I had more than one pair of my own shoes in the bag. The message is clear: Don't get too sidetracked putting myself in another's energy and life. Focus on my own path. Walk my own yellow brick road.

Mom, I sent you the daisy. I didn't tell you before, but it was our private moment. Had you known about it, there would have been an expectation associated with receiving the vision.

As in most things, expectations mess us up. Expectations imprison us in self-imposed limitations. Perhaps so much more would have been possible if we had been in a more open, allowing state. Allowing is so different. Whatever comes is welcome; it is well, it is right. Especially in relationships, and in the roles we assume, allowing shakes off our rigid beliefs that entrench our values.

It strikes me that we were going to write a play about visits from people of other ages to Socrates's cell in the last month of his life. Wouldn't a main theme be freedom and what truly constitutes a free person?

It gets me thinking that perhaps he displayed true freedom by being true to his beliefs, by not choosing to flee or to accept exile. A truly free man doesn't take the easy way out; he is diligent and truthful to his being, his morals. Maybe in our own way, we're writing the play right now.

CHAPTER 14

My obsession to build my business was all about reaching my goal to provide for my children. That narrow focus gave side rails to rub up against that kept me on side when I threatened to head off the rails.

What threatened me? Exhaustion. Self-pity. Fear and doubt. What encouraged me to keep going? My happy customers. Grandma. Faith. My staff. My love of the products we made and knowing that they mattered.

Imagine, Clo, 18 years of pushing. I sat down one day—a day when you were across from me asleep on the couch, with Mia on your belly—and wrote down 18 chapter headings for the 18 years I ran GEG. Want to see them?

Yeah, baby!

Okay, here goes.

18 Chapter Headings for 18 Years of GEG

Why, Not How

Soup or Salad?

Bootstrapping

The Three *B*s

When No Means Yes

At the Gym

Hug and Reward

Blame It on Dopamine

Risky Business

I'll Be Faithful, I Promise

Choosing Wisely

The Four Can Quota

When Yes Means No

Hop On, Hop Off

VW and Other Vehicles

Follow the Nudge

Tools

As Happy Is to Happiness, Busy Is To …

I have a humble suggestion. You have too many headings. Why not pare it down to 12? AA did it. The apostles did it. Why not GEG?

Eliminate six headings? All right, here goes.

12 Chapter Headings for GEG

Why, Not How

Soup or Salad?

Bootstrapping

Risky Business

I'll Be Faithful, I Promise

When No Means Yes

Hug and Reward

At the Gym

Blame It on Dopamine

The Four Can Quota

When Yes Means No

Tools

I like that. More manageable. Thank you. Okay, now, what do they mean?

The first heading is perhaps the most powerful. It's what carried me all the way through. This may sound a bit like I'm giving a lecture, but I want this bit to be clear so that if someone wants to start a business, she can write these headings down and try to elaborate on each one. Sort of a working tool for working moms.

Why, Not How

I had no idea how I would make a bootstrapped granola business work. I had no how. I had no business plan. I had no plan of any kind. I simply had a powerful why. Why am I doing this?

Like many single working mothers, my motivation was to provide for my children. That strong why helped me stay focused through the tough times. I learned that the why really matters, and it can't simply be "to make money."

A why has to have legs. It has to have a feel, a taste, a smell. Mine was to hand each child a key to the house we would eventually own so they always had a true north to come home to. I visualized the bright red front door.

The ways and means of how will constantly present themselves. You won't have to go looking for them. The how evolves daily.

Sometimes it may stumble. Sometimes it may soar. It will be many things, but it will never be static. The why never changes.

Establishing that strong why helps establish the guiding principles of corporate culture—what goods or services to supply, how to treat staff, the treatment of suppliers, everything. Good how decisions are harmonious with your why. They feel right. Step-by-step, your business dream will become reality.

Soup or Salad?

Your business is a public reflection of the private you. It's more than just your preference for soup or salad, red or white. It's the Rembrandt or the cat. What are your beliefs? The house is burning—what do you grab? What matters more, love, or money? Although simplistic, "Soup or Salad?" reminds us to spend time understanding our values. Some are tribal, and some are personal. All are capable of scrutiny and change.

The public self is the one who shows up for Sunday dinner with the family. The private self is curled up on the couch with a book. The secret self cries herself to sleep.

It's easy to say, "Leave your stuff at the door." I say bring it in, unpack it and use it to enrich the workplace and the work. Work it out before you take it out on others. Whatever lingers in your emotional baggage will come out in the course of a day.

A master breeds masters. A leader breeds leaders. And a crook breeds crooks. Know thyself.

Bootstrapping

Bootstrapping simply refers to lifting yourself up by the bootstraps and starting a business without incurring debt. Ten years after starting the business, I was informed that my business was actually modelled after a specific strategy. That was news to me. I thought it was the result of 80 percent desperation and 20 percent inspiration.

Here are some ins and outs of bootstrapping a business.

- Your product has a short repeat cycle.
- The unit price is low enough for clients to pay rapidly.
- Forget perfectionism at the starting gate—it takes too long.
- Choose customers who can pay their bills.
- No borrowing means no debt. Consider yourself already a millionaire.
- Be wary of the receivable that, if not paid, could bankrupt you.
- Keep credit cycle short, only shipping the next order when the previous one is paid.
- You're the jack of all trades, and you do your own accounting.
- Accept slow growth.

- Because every purchase is financed with your cash flow, no cash means no purchase.

- Focus on why you're doing this.

- Keep your steps small, and keep stepping.

- Only do what you really believe in. People will sense that and want to be a part of it.

- Keep packaging simple. Less is more.

- Don't expect anything from anyone.

- Ask for guidance from your higher self. Ask, ask, ask.

- Bring the kids in and show them what you're doing.

- Eat, sleep and breathe your venture.

- Remember that venture and adventure are close cousins.

- Repeat often that "small is beautiful." One day you'll believe it.

- Breathe.

That's enough for tonight, okay? Clo, you there?

I think I lost her. She's an artist, after all. This entrepreneurship stuff is a bit dry.

Bonne nuit, Cherie.

CHAPTER 15

Bootstrapping almost seems out of place in the world of business terminological hegemonization. Dazed? Seriously, bootstrapping is a homey, folksy word in a fancy and formal business universe that takes itself very seriously. Mom, you'd look good in those big, utilitarian farm boots, lugging around hay and feeding chickens. Ha!

Why do I equate picking yourself up by the boots with farming? I'm not sure, but maybe it's because when the kids were threatened with no future, you focused on getting them fed. Actually, a granola business was a smart thing. Even when there was no other food in the house, there was granola. Sometimes we ate it twice a day. We didn't make it easy, did we? Which kids do?

How did you guess about the prostituting thing? I told you I had a part-time job cleaning houses.

I knew because out of nowhere, you had some spending money. New underwear was showing up in the laundry basket. You'd come home with pastries and cosmetics.

Remember that guy Andrew? I was pissed because he wouldn't pay me. He wanted sex but wouldn't pay for it.

As the expression goes, they always pay for it one way or another. And we often prostitute ourselves, sometimes for security, sometimes out of loneliness or neediness, whatever.

I only did it for about seven months. I figured I loved sex, so why not get paid for it?

How did that work for you?

It didn't with Andrew. He never paid up.

Was the sex any good?

It was amazing!

I remember thinking, "What if I ask her, and I'm wrong? What a horrible thing to accuse her of." Meanwhile, it was true. Maybe that's why I never brought it up: because I knew it was true and didn't want to have it confirmed to me.

I remember being so horrified, humiliated, disgusted, ashamed—all those things rolled into one when I realized what you were doing. Now, it's just part of the craziness that was your life. I never brought it up, and you never admitted it. It was one more awful realization to live with. My brilliant Chloe …

Drop it.

So you like the term bootstrapping?

It describes you well. I did help you, right at the beginning when I was 8, remember?

I do. You were using the mixer, and it was the same height as you. It weighed the same too. You had the drive, the focus.

I also remember the poetry slam you organized. You were about 17 then. That was the absolute coolest event. All these people showed up at the art gallery you had rented, and they brought instruments, including their voices. You all made the most amazing, impromptu music—or whatever you could call it. It was a powerful, creative event that blew me away. Bravo, Clo.

Thanks, Mom. I remember you rallied, helped me bring all the stuff we needed and stayed for the event. It was awesome. I did other ones too that you didn't know about. But I was doing drugs, and things started to get unhinged.

That's an understatement.

I'm so sorry. I was a nightmare. I was sick, Mom.

You were sick, Clo. You had so much potential. Remember the five-page poem you wrote without using the letter *e*? I wish I could find it. It was brilliant.

That was hard to do. No the, *no* me, *no* yes *or* agree *or* tree. *It made sense too.*

It made a lot of sense. It was extraordinary.

Thanks.

You're welcome, my lovely one. I went to hear BJ Miller speak last night at McGill. He's the physician who is associated with the Zen Hospice Project in San Francisco. It's a tiny palliative care facility with just six beds. Then he went on TED. Now, he's spending his time speaking about palliative care around the world.

"Less horrible—more wonderful." I loved that line. That's the perspective he wants to bring to dying. He spoke about how the system needs a redesign to be more people-centred. Death needs to shift to a civic issue. It definitely affects 100 percent of us, so we need to have a dialogue about it. We need to design for it. I agreed with him totally and spoke to him afterwards.

I wish I could tell everyone that it's really all good, that wonderful things do happen after death and that no one dies. We simply leave the room. Clo, do you think that's gonna happen?

Mom, we're making that happen right now. This conversation is going to grow.

I really hope so. It would give people so much relief and hope, bring them peace.

Tell me more about BJ.

He makes me think of the question, "Do you have the courage to live the dream that picked you?"

A dream picked him. When he was in college, he messed around with friends on the top of a parked train car and was electrocuted. He lost two legs and half an arm. He slowly recovered and eventually became a doctor. Living near death for so long attracted him to palliative care, and he has become a very vocal advocate for bringing good care to the forefront. The need is great. His courage is inspiring.

Talk about bootstrapping—about picking yourself up, dusting yourself off and starting all over again.

He goes through this horrific accident and then becomes BJ after the accident, as opposed to BJ before the accident. They're two different people. He's always comparing himself to the old BJ. Then one day, he stops comparing and simply accepts himself as he is: limbless, different. He begins to see himself as whole.

Coinciding with this personal process is the work he's doing within the medical system to help galvanize a shift towards whole-patient care, patient-centred care, whole-person care. There are several terms describing the same thing.

The palliative experience is so many different things. Joanne B. had barely eight hours with her father in palliative care. She remembers that time fondly. She also lost a son suddenly and tragically, and she has still not accepted his death five years after the fact.

Irene P. had four months in palliative care, accompanying her husband. She would be there every day without fail. She too recognizes the value of accompanying her life partner, bringing dignity and love to his last days as his body broke down.

Each experience is unique in its makeup but universal in its inevitability. So why aren't we addressing this issue front and centre? Because the medical profession is set up to cure, to fix and to treat—not to accompany and offer quality of life and the relief of suffering.

Miller wants to see all that change. I want to see people have more affinity for the process and less aversion. We need to talk about this. We need to express our wishes, to converse while we're healthy and well and can choose for ourselves. We also need to let go of the concept of burdenhood.

Every activity works both ways. The giver and the receiver are both receiving and giving. The energy flows back and forth. There are only receivers who give to each other. We do not become burdens when we get sick. We become opportunities for those we love to step up.

I like the word receiver because it is like being a radio receiver tuned to a frequency. Yesterday, after meditating, my body was vibrating so intensely that I put my hand on my solar plexus and experienced the physical sensation of deep, powerful vibration emanating from that region. My receiver was tuned in to some incredibly high frequency. Minutes later, it calmed down, and I was able to get on with my day.

How about I continue past bootstrapping?

On!

Risky Business

How much risk is too much risk? When it keeps you up at night. When does it keep you up at night? No one can answer that but you. Risk-assessment models abound, but the bottom line is that the ability to manage uncertainty with a cool head is personal and different for each of us. It is also the key feature of a good leader. It's easy to lead in the good times. It's essential to lead calmly in bad ones.

Here's a quick assessment tool that helped me to evaluate "Should I or shouldn't I?"

"What is the worst thing that could happen if I make this choice?"

If I can live with that possible outcome, I go for it. If not, thanks but no thanks. Assessing risk and handling uncertainty are two inevitable realities of entrepreneurship.

Here's another gem from Sue that she attributes to Aristotle. "If you don't want to be criticized, say nothing, do nothing, be nothing." Entrepreneurship is feeling the fear and doing it anyway.

Entrepreneurship, from the French word entreprendre, which means to undertake. Oh, the magic of wordsmithing. The undertaker prepares bodies for burial or cremation. I vote to change your title from entrepreneur to profounder. A founder of a business who looks for the pros in each situation, capitalizes on them and turns opportunity into success.

An entrepreneur is a profounder. I've heard that expression from my wise friend Alex. Love it.

I'll Be Faithful, I Promise!

Who to trust? According to the Quebec Bar Foundation, there are three main requirements to any legitimate contract.

- There is an exchange of consent; handshakes are valid.
- The parties are capable of contracting.
- The contract has a particular object.

Character, not contract, guarantees proper fulfilment of the terms. If a handshake won't suffice, an inch of written contract and an army of lawyers won't protect. That said, breaking up is hard to do. A contract is for the breakup, not the marriage. A simple contract between partners before anyone imagines the possibility of conflict can save expensive and draining legal battles.

Naiveté never served me well in business. It never served in any areas of my life. Smarten up, ladies. Stop depending on a man, playing small and doing the damsel in distress routine. Learn the rules of the game, align with people of integrity and protect yourselves.

When No Means Yes

Selling is being ready for potential rejection with every sales call. These two strategies helped me.

- "Every no is just a yes in disguise." Celebrate the no. Rejoice in the rejection. Know that a yes is coming just around the next corner. This mindset is enough to shift your energy to a more positive place. Some prospects will never buy. Some will take years. Some will place an order on the first visit. This non-verbal, deliberate thought kept me in the game and kept potential clients with long adoption cycles on my horizons.

- "If you want to buy, buy. If you don't want to buy, bye-bye." This other non-verbal, personal mind game kept me confident and presented an energy of success even when I felt discouraged. If my product isn't a good fit, it isn't a good sale. Think long-term.

The only way to really know what's going on is to get out and see for yourself. Tack this mantra to your computer screen: "Sell, sell, sell." Without sales, nothing else is possible. Profit is not a dirty word. You're bootstrapping. Without profit, there is no business.

As John Le Carré said, "A desk is a dangerous place from which to view the world."

If I can succeed in turning a rejection into a motivation, then I'm an alchemist. There is huge power in doing this, not just in business but in all of life.

It's about being a pro founder and a pro finder.

Clever. Clo, get this. John comes for dinner last night. It is delicious, intimate and wonderful. The meal, the conversation, the passionate embrace—everything. It's like nothing I've ever experienced.

Then this morning, not even a "good morning." Not even a hello or a thank-you by text. As my ego kicks in and I'm feeling hurt, I breathe and send a short note saying good morning around 10:30. He responds by saying how busy he is.

Andrea, don't react. Stay self-contained, live just the present moment and don't inflate your sense of hurt. Maybe he's troubled by something completely unrelated. Remember Sue's words: "Everyone writes her own fiction. Get out of the weeds. You have no idea why he's acting this way." Practice non-reactivity. Allow this hurt to float by and let it go. Turn a no into a yes.

I'm at my mom's now and pull *The Untethered Soul* by Michael Singer from her bookcase. Upon randomly opening to page 132, I read, "You will be aware that each moment of each day is unfolding and you neither have control, nor crave it." Singer reminds me to be a witness. Perfect words for today. Thank you, Mr. Singer.

Mom, considering you want to stay in the cottage for the summer, keeping things light and easy will serve you. If it gets tense, just take off up north. You're moving beyond acceptance—a tough lesson in itself—to something even tougher: detachment.

Look at the title of the book: untethered is something that is detached. This is evolution speeded up, Mom. Acceptance took a few years. Things like patience and non-judgement were a piece of cake compared to acceptance. But detachment goes to a whole other level of wise living. The drama affects you a lot less—not because you've numbed it with alcohol or drugs, but because you've chosen to be a witness to it. Big, Mom. Big.

Detachment. I like that. I have the perfect book in my hands to fully explore the concept. I was drawn to that book on the shelf. At first my eyes went up to the bookcase, and I saw *Living with Joy*, my old favourite. But then my eyes glanced at the book beside it, and I just knew: "Ah, that's the one."

Detachment—a state of objectivity, aloofness. Detachment also means a troop, a squad, a unit sent on a separate mission. We are meant to detach eventually from our relationships, yet we put so much energy into creating them. They give meaning to our lives. They create a framework by which to navigate the outside world. We put all this effort into creating them just to evolve to a state of detachment from them. No wonder living consciously is not a simple task. It is deliberate.

I lived detached by detaching my brain. Many others do the same. That is what we accomplish by having those so-called mental illnesses. We detach from the norms of society. Don't have to work. Don't have to observe the rules of etiquette or even how to cross a street safely. We detach so much that our personal hygiene goes to shit.

I've seen that.

That's just the obvious outer manifestation. We live in other worlds so intricate, so complex in their relationships that they're real to us. We become detached from your world and attached to the worlds in our head. They are even more real to us than yours are to you because they are condensed, closer than our own noses. Those voices are with us constantly. That's why we need the drugs and the cigarettes: they provide a momentary lapse from the noise in our heads—relief for a nanosecond.

Interesting. And terrible. How exhausting.

Mom, I saw the world happening around me, but I was not a part of it anymore. It was my choice and my destiny, and I was living on purpose. You have a Course in Miracles *now. What are you going to do with it?*

I'm going to read it and study it.

Good. There were several attempts made to get you to read it, but each time you set up a roadblock. No more roadblocks, okay?

Okay.

Happy Mother's Day. Two years of caring for a sick Clo. That cycle is complete. Your role is completed with me. Be aware to complete it with Daniel. Matthew still needs you as a toddler needs his mother.

Got it.

Clo, I read *Ten Thousand Miles without a Cloud* by Sun Shuyun. It's the story of Xuanzang, a Chinese Buddhist monk who lived centuries ago. Xuanzang made an 18-year journey overland to India and back to learn about the origins of Buddhism. Detachment is a major theme of the book. Shuyun writes, "True freedom comes from releasing your personal history. The actions of others, the moods, the play, the consequences, the drama."

Hug and Reward

HR stands for hug and reward, not human resources. How to hire the right person? I have absolutely no idea. One thing I do know is that we all need appreciation and encouragement. Start from there. Appreciate them and give your team the space to dazzle you.

Growing your staff is a linear process like the rest of your business. Not all lines are straight, so expect some missteps, but encourage excellence and watch what happens.

There is no such thing as unskilled labour. Every labour requires skill and moves towards constant improvement. The dishwasher is as important as the chef.

You actually hugged your staff almost every morning. Every single one of them. That is so cool, Mom.

In some cultures, hugging is not acceptable. It took some staff a while to warm up to this level of contact. Once they did, they were the best huggers of all, as if they had been craving it all along. That was how I motivated my gang: by authentically loving them.

Possessed people run away from hugs. We run away from affection. Malevolent spirits lose their energy around affection. Therein lies the key to reducing the space they occupy in people's consciousness. Fill that space with love, and they feel squeezed out. Never stop trying to hug that person, even as they do everything to push you away.

I lived that too.

At the Gym

What soul qualities am I developing in this situation? You may not have time to exercise, but starting a business is like hitting the gym every single day. All that pushback against the obstacles in front of you creates toning, like lifting weights. Every single day, there's something to challenge you, forcing you to dig deep.

When the worst possible thing happens, and you survive, you come out the other side realizing it wasn't the worst thing; it was, in fact, a gift. And as sure as the sun will rise the next day, the tough stuff will come knocking at your door once more.

Going to the gym. Going to the gym. Wash, rinse, repeat. The obstacles become challenges. The paradox is that by making your way past obstacles, the path of least resistance opens up.

I really like this one about using resistance to build your resilience muscle. The problem about being so resilient is that one becomes an island. You did it. I did it. We're tough. We feel we can do it alone. We don't reach out to others. We're independent and hard-headed, and we could have been assisted more. After all, when you have a company, you don't do it alone, correct? You're accompanied.

I think I'm going to steal some of your material. You're clever. And seriously, you're right. There were times I should have asked for help and didn't.

Blame It on Dopamine

It takes a lot of energy to build a business from nothing. True, low dopamine levels in the brain will make a person feel lethargic. If you're feeling like your battery is low, check your diet, hours of sleep, and level of exercise. The quality of the air you breathe and the water you drink matter too. Once all those check out okay, the missing ingredient may be more emotional than physical.

In order to move beyond doubt and build self-confidence, try the quick-hit or quick-win strategy. Athletes do it. Actors do it. Entrepreneurs can do it too. Take on something doable. Sell to the "low-lying fruit" customer, the easy sell. Build your confidence, and then shoot for a bigger one.

Quick hits and quick wins give you that "Yes!" sensation. By deliberately setting up your smaller victories, you build the confidence to venture forth to bigger and bigger ones.

As for getting in shape physically, my top five brain feeders every day are:

- Break the fast with the juice of a lemon in warm water
- One tablespoon of apple cider vinegar half an hour before each meal
- One tablespoon of unsulphured blackstrap molasses per day
- At least one salad per day
- Forget alcohol

Mom, I would add:

- *Stay away from all drugs—recreational, medicinal, over the counter, under the counter, around the counter*
- *Swim*
- *Do smiling yoga*

I like the smiling yoga. I can even do that while driving.

The greatest tool we all have is the energy that flows within us. How well it flows is up to us. On page 44 of *The Untethered*

Soul, Singer puts it simply and beautifully: "Energy doesn't get old, it doesn't get tired and it doesn't need food. What it needs is openness and receptivity … openness allows energy in, closing blocks the flow. You choose."

CHAPTER 16

It's 7:00 a.m., and John and I are having coffee together. We still don't actually spend the night together, so it's nice to reconvene in the morning. We discuss important domestic issues like how the ducks are getting along and whether I saw the muskrat yesterday. He points out that the wind's blowing down from the north today. Because we're perched on the south shore of this island, it blows over our heads towards the lake, allowing the waters of this bay to be still while decent waves form three hundred yards off shore.

"Look further than outside the window to know if it's a good sailing day," he says. Good advice for life, no? Although the sky is completely overcast, he predicts a sunny day. Hmm, I'm not so sure. By late morning, the skies are clear.

How do you feel about John? You're not sleeping over?

Like every relationship, stuff comes up. If I can stay non-reactive, it evolves. We're gradually getting to know each other. I don't hide this conversation from him, so part of him thinks I'm crazy, and part thinks I'm wonderful.

Sounds like a normal relationship to me.

You're funny. He told me he's bipolar, and that threw me off for a moment. He controls it with lithium and has taken his meds fastidiously for the last 30 years. His honesty blows me away.

He's candid about his confusion over women, his relationships and the pace of life. He's got such a big heart, Clo. The other morning we were gardening, and this young woman stopped her bike just in front of us. She was struggling with a bag that kept sliding off the back of her bike. He went over there with a bungee cord, secured her bag and wished her a great day.

I like the unintended irony of that previous bit. He thinks you're crazy and wonderful. Sounds like he is too.

Unintended irony—nice phrase. Why does love have to be so complicated?

So why aren't you sleeping over?

Because I like to wake up at 4:30 a.m. and write. Because it's the last bit of space we keep from each other. Because our bedtime habits are so different. Because I'm keeping a small grain of independence. Satisfied?

Not really.

That's all you're getting.

I've been rummaging through random old scribbles, and I found these words that I wrote about you a couple of years ago.

> It has come down to this. No more chasing her down streets, rummaging through her bag for drugs, waiting for police, going to the police station to file a missing person's report or flying off to all points everywhere to find her, rescue her and take her to hospital. This is the last hospital stop.
>
> No more visits to the justice building to make a court appearance and plead the case of why she should be committed for 30 days for an evaluation. Nothing was worse than that. Nothing. The stenographer and the security guard had to help me up off the floor after I collapsed. I actually collapsed, sobbing in public. Never did that ever before or since.
>
> How many admissions in all? I lost count after 12. Must be around 20 by now. No more screaming and swearing. No more erratic speech or crazy, jerky motions. No more fuck-offs. So much clashing with Chloe and her demons all the time.

It was really rough, Clo.

I am eternally sorry for causing you so much grief.

I know. And now, here you are so loving, helpful, attentive and grateful. Talk about unintended irony. Talk about crazy and wonderful.

Let me tell you about my life. I actually do think I was born incoherent. I wanted to experiment, but it got ahead of me. I couldn't stop the slippery slide once it had gathered momentum. Things like recreational drug use, the wrong friends, a nature that was so impetuous, a lack of clarity, mental mayhem—these all contributed to create the perfect storm of psychosis.

There were times in the psych ward when I didn't even know where I was. I mean days. I remember seeing you through the glass, and I'd have a split second of recognition. Then nothing. I didn't know you. I remembered your face but couldn't quite place you. Yet I couldn't forget giving five-dollar blowjobs to buy a coffee and a muffin.

Oh, God.

You really knew how to keep it together. I look at you today and see someone with it all together, and I wonder at the strength of the tools you use.

They're almost the same ones you used to stay alive, to do whatever you had to do to survive. I simply pointed mine in a positive direction, not a self-destructive one.

The difference is I truly had a deep knowing that I am loved. I am the recipient of the constant well-being that the universe is sending out to us all. This knowing helped me feel I was never alone. It brought me back when I felt despair.

Probably the most important tool I have is my knowing. Not a faith, but a knowing that all is as it should be. The universe is perfect. The higher power that is the stage manager of this crazy dance called life on earth doesn't make errors. To get to that point of knowing and accepting that all is as it should be means I have to limit my exposure to all that is.

If I watch the news every night, the evidence will be overwhelming that things are completely insane. I'll sink into outrage, despair and denouncement of much that I witness. Instead, I don't turn on the TV. I limit my exposure to the news. I try to gaze upon beauty, to be a witness to my troubles and the stresses of life. That way, I can put some energy into imagining things as I wish them to be. My mind isn't all cluttered up with things "as they presently are." And then, that vibration attracts like vibration to itself, and gradually my life shifts to become my imaginings. It is like imagining miracles and then allowing them in. They do present themselves.

Share, share …

But I want to hear more of your story.

Okay. I was heading into oblivion of drugs, crime and prostitution, using and being abused by so-called friends. I knew it was happening, but I lost the ability to fight it. I came out of it a few times, balled my eyes out and realized what a mess I had created—but I wasn't able to get out. No matter the great team around me and the love of family, my destiny was to mess up totally, to give everyone the opportunity to rise to their best selves and then exit. I did.

Yes, you did.

There was no way anything could have been different. It was not up to you or anyone else; it wasn't in your control. But you got that, you knew that. You knew you only controlled yourself, so at some point you stopped feeling guilty.

That took work, lots of deliberate thought to tell myself to let go of guilt.

There seems to be this strange pressure around us to feel guilt and shame. What a waste.

I was so relieved for you that the trauma ended. I had given you all I had and so felt no guilt. All was as it should be.

Still, nothing could ever prepare me to witness your inanimate body. That scene is forever burnt in my memory. The towel under your chin. Your eyes wide open. The pasty colour of your skin. The coldness of your skin in contrast to the burning fever of the previous night. The weirdness of the automatic bed that raised your chest as if you were breathing until I pulled the plug on the bed. For an instant, I felt like I was pulling the plug on you. I couldn't leave you. I couldn't leave the room. I couldn't take my eyes off you, as if I was wondering if maybe there was some mistake. It was hard to believe you had actually taken leave of your body. I wanted to remember those beautiful fingers, the freckles, your nose—everything.

I remembered your battles. You fought two big illnesses. There were certain things I never could get used to. With the cancer, it was that you went to bed so early every night. No friends, no parties, no nothing. Just a huge cocktail of meds and off to bed by 8:00 p.m.

With the psychosis, it was that you were in a prison of the mind, stuck in a locked-down psych ward, the beautiful summer months passing you by. Coming off a crack-induced high, screaming, jerking your head and body, possessed.

Can we talk about this possession thing? It is actually possession by a non-physical entity. Sometimes the voices came from several entities. Remember how they used to make you physically sick?

They made me really ill. I remember throwing up, not being able to drive and having to fight off nausea and fatigue.

Their energy is so warped that they screw up the physical world. Like those gnarly trees, they deform and deface. They deformed my thoughts, defaced my peace, possessed me right up until the blessed moment I left my body.

The strange thing is that the relationship became a dependence, and I could no sooner get rid of this haunting than cut off my own nose. We had an agreement that he would stay till I left my body. So even when you tried to get him to leave, I resisted and kept him close. Why? Because I was so cut off from regular life, from friends, from work or play or anything normal. All I had was him and smoking. They were my two companions. Both were disgusting to you, making you sick. But both were real to me. Make no mistake, Ma, they were real. We had a real contract, and we are both free now.

So a foreign entity actually took possession of you?

I wouldn't call them foreign.

What would you call them, then?

Him, actually. It was a male energy. His name was Zack. I called him Zacko because he made me wacko. I know that sounds dumb, but it's true. He changed his name a lot to keep me unbalanced. It's kind of like a sick friend continuously badgering, being critical and hateful, swearing and yelling at me. He gave me no peace, but he also was the only real company I had. I hated and loved him at the same time, like a child who is really attached to a cruel, abusive parent. The parent gives just enough love to keep you close. Then he terrorizes by molesting and beating, and when you're at the brink of breaking, he tells you it's for your own good, and he quiets down. It's diabolical.

And yet your real parents loved you so much. Your grandparents too.

He was with me many lifetimes, Mom. He was all I had when everything else dropped away. I had you guys, but you belonged to a different land—the land of the living. I was in the land of the drifting. At the end, I was in a different land too. You called that the land of the dying.

And I knew you resented us being in the land of the living while you were in the land of the dying. And were they ever two different lands! A person could move between them, but you resented that. If I had a phone call and was having a happy conversation, you tried to reduce the interaction to a state of chaos with your chaotic talk.

It became so difficult that I gave up trying to navigate both worlds, stopped all forms of social interaction, shaved my head as a sign of deep personal pain, and chose to inhabit the land of the dying with you. Days slowed, and time stood still. Only time continued to move for you. Slowly, slowly, you faded and dropped away until just the breath was left. The first and last act of life—the breath.

I sit here now by the water's edge and contemplate how much we do to avoid realizing the fact that we are all simply slowly approaching death. Every human we see will be dead within pretty much a hundred years. Every one.

I learned about fibreglass from John and discovered another blessed metaphor. Remember, Clo, how we compiled lists of metaphors? Fibreglass. We consider it to be tough, strong and durable. Yet through the process of osmosis, water can slowly penetrate the gel coat, the hard exterior finish that everyone thinks is impenetrable. That finish is actually porous. Water creates blisters that bubble up the fibreglass. In order to get them out, much like a cancer, they have to be dug out with a knife. One has to ensure to remove the bubble completely, refilling the space with epoxy. We are like that fibreglass, aren't we?

Another sailor metaphor: the plight of Laser Canada. It illustrates the failure of humans to recognize the inevitable. In this case, the inevitable reality is that boats don't wear out very fast. As demand for new Laser boats skyrocketed, the company opened up manufacturing plants around the world. Once that demand was satisfied, capital investments lay underutilized, leading eventually to bankruptcy for Laser. They went, according to John, "1,000 mph right into a wall." Sounds like our civilization.

Sounds like me.

Yup. Sometimes, writing to you brings up many feelings of loss. I seem to be like the incoming tide: get up close to acceptance, wash over detachment and then recede back to grief, loss and self-pity. Then I rise again, a little closer this time, and accept a little more.

Mom, let's get back to business. Where were we?

We're at the Four Can Quota.

The Four Can Quota

Isaac Smith raises magnificent, grass-fed, Red Angus cows in Mabou, Nova Scotia. When he's out in the fields, they follow him around; he whistles, and they come running. They're smart, gracious and intimidating in their hugeness.

When I drive down his long, private lane, the calves playfully run alongside the car as if to say, "Game on."

From my friend Isaac, who is a 15-hour drive from my place, I learned the importance of the four can quota.

That was the amount of milk he could ship daily from his small dairy farm. Four cans of eight gallons each. That was it. The back seat came out of his '65 Comet, and the cans went in. Then it was doing chores, and the day was done. Every day, a four can quota.

Isaac speaks with fondness of his 2,300-pound bull named Red Milestone Suji. What a name. He describes how he didn't want that bull initially because of his size. It's tough to control a recalcitrant bull. Turns out, Suji was anything but tough. He was a pussycat. Why? Because from a young age, he'd been haltered and shown at fairs. He was gentle and fertile. Isaac recalls one Easter weekend when nine calves were born, the heifers all fertilized by big Suji.

Several times, when I just needed the open road to clear my head, I looked no further for the geographical cure than Isaac's house. Watching him talk to his cows, feed his cats or ride the tractor brought home to me the true heroism of everyday life. It's in the acts of the mundane that the divine is recognizable.

Once I learned that, I took it easier on myself and stopped trying to find my enlightened life's purpose that would bring me fame and fortune. It wasn't my business card that would show the measure of me. It was in being able to manage all the balls that were in the air simultaneously. That was enough.

That one's my new favourite heading and content. I remember meeting Isaac and how gracious he was. He was generous too. What a spot—Mabou, Nova Scotia.

It's about seeing the divine in the sublime and the heroism of everyday life. This may not seem like a benchmark lesson from 18 years of running a business, but it is to me. GEG was a divine endeavour. The products mattered. The staff mattered. The work mattered.

Chapter 17

My Diary: February 13, 2016—The Liberation of Shame

Chloe is dying. I still want to exercise. I still want to have my hair cut in a funky style. I still want to buy a soft yellow cashmere sweater to wear with my jeans this spring. I still want to go snowshoeing this morning, to meditate, to build a fire, to read my favourite books and to write.

I still want to continue the conversation with an interesting, sensitive man I just met. I really want to do that. I still want to laugh, have fun and rejoice in living. All this I still want to do, even as I'm caring every day for Chloe. I love caring for Chloe. I wouldn't choose to be anywhere else. What I'm realizing is that I want the other things too. And I want to enjoy them without feeling shameful about being happy in my life. That is my choice.

Chloe, I love you, I grieve for you, I cry for you and I wish for all your suffering to end. I will always have you with me in my heart. I understand that your journey in this body is almost over. For two years you've battled surgery, chemotherapy, masses of drugs and natural remedies. We dipped our toes in many rivers. They have all flowed to this one spot, to the now where you can no longer dress yourself, walk unassisted or eat.

I would remove your suffering if I could, yet I know that there is some good reason for all of this. Everything is a miracle to me—all life matters and works as an intricate, interwoven machine. There are no wrong pieces.

Some things I know, and some things I believe. I know there is only life. I know there is no death. I know this because I had a direct experience of death in December 1991. From that moment onwards, I have been unafraid of death.

I believe that all is as it should be. I believe that from the perspective of your oversoul, your life work has accomplished what you set out to accomplish. You explored madness, addiction and depths of depravity. You were the catalyst for us to either open our hearts or reject you. You gave us that choice. And you didn't make yourself lovable; you made it tough. You lied, stole, cheated, prostituted yourself, swore at us, disappeared for days, threw away many chances and abused your body. You spent days, even months, in the psych ward. I was so despairing that I almost gave up on you several times. But I simply couldn't. You were my precious Chloe, and I didn't want to find out you had died behind a dumpster, alone and abused.

And then you returned. By no means converted and angelic,

you were still that demonic, addicted, psychotic rebel. But at least I knew where you were. At least I could contact you, bring you a chai latte and visit if only for a minute. Sometimes it took half an hour to find parking. I'd go up to the ward, and you'd be so rude and mean, swearing at me and threatening to throw things at me that I wouldn't stay. I learned to stay calm, to assert that I was not comfortable being spoken to that way and that I would be back. Hopefully next time things would be better.

Always there was hope. Sometimes they were better. Sometimes not. It was long, frustrating and painful. No rewards, hugs or thank-yous. Just my own sense that I would keep my heart open and show you love without any condition of you acting a certain way. Aha—unconditional love is finally part of my experience. I now know what it is.

We carry beliefs about how we should act when someone is dying. Should we wear black? Should we be sad? What about having fun? Is it even possible?

For me, solitude helps a lot. One day a week, I sequester myself away with my books, my computer and miles of snowy trails to snowshoe. That is my therapy. I can soak in a bath, burn logs in the fireplace and stay in my PJs all day if I choose. I choose. That is the secret.

So I'm choosing life-affirming stuff: exercise, eating right and drinking lots of water. I have a real problem drinking hospital water. I'm not sure if others feel this way, but I don't want to drink their water. It's as if by drinking it, I'll catch whatever is happening in the corridors and rooms. So on Saturdays, I drink, which creates its own dilemma of course. Can't go out when I need a bathroom every hour. Unlike guys, the great outdoors is not our toilet!

I've just focused on John, whom I met a few days ago. Haven't met yet in person. Pulled the reversed five of cups. A clear yes! It's a time to be hopeful, with new prospects; I just came out of a difficult situation, and all is now possible. No more need to twist myself into a pretzel for love.

Just called Chloe. I can't complain that her dad is forgetting to give her the meds! She slurs her words and tells me, "I'm passing all my diseases over to the vet."

"Okay," I say. "See you tomorrow."

For someone who always wanted to take drugs, she's certainly getting a taste of the grade-A stuff. I need to be a bit irreverent around death. I need to mock it a bit, to feel some kind of one-upmanship over it. I'm not sure why, but that helps.

My Diary: February 15, 2016

All you ingested yesterday was ice chips and clear chicken broth. Then you threw up. When the throwing up happens, you throw up tons of black liquid. Black. What is that? Internal bleeding?

The palliative care ward is life's swinging door in motion.

Life's in and out basket. People here will really come and go from your life. You meet a patient. You get close to family members. Within minutes, the shared experience bonds strangers. And then, as happened yesterday, the patient dies. Last night when I left, someone's mother, grandmother or sister was in the next room. This morning I arrive, and she's gone. All those family members are gone too, vanished. The vigil is over.

I glance in the room next door. An elderly man sleeps alone. He sleeps with his mouth wide open, his thin and pale skin pulled taut over his cheek bones. I'm alarmed that there is no one with him. He seems to exude a man who is busy doing something. I say he's preparing his journey, reviewing his life and planning his death.

Another thing I noticed today is how people want to know the gossip. They want to know what is wrong, where it started, how long it's been, how is she managing with all that pain. I don't feel like sharing any of that information. It's off-limits, end of story.

To ask every day, "How is Chloe?" is to not understand the slow death process. More people should have it explained to them. Like living fully, dying fully takes time.

To the medical system, a patient is a set of givens. Past medical history, age, sex, race, habits, current illness and symptoms are treated as titbits of information to help the staff determine which cocktail of drugs is appropriate, which other treatments apply, et cetera. To the family, the patient is a loved one. Full stop. We just want suffering to end. Another full stop.

They gave you multiple blood transfusions. Why? Because you were a level-3 patient, which means "resuscitate and treat." If you had been classified a level-4 patients, then it's "provide comfort and minimize pain"—a palliative approach. It is a designated protocol, not a subjective decision of how to treat. Note to self: it's important that the person has the correctly-designated level.

My Diary: February 16, 2016

Just picked up the *Globe and Mail* from January 23. Takes me time to get around to reading the paper. I stumble upon an article on Janet Bannister, a partner at Real Ventures and a true champion of Canadian entrepreneurship.

What strikes me the most is her description of her father. He gave her unconditional love and support; from there, she thrived. This is what people need so that they thrive, so that they believe in themselves, so that they know they have meaning and value.

Whether they create a company of a thousand employees or one with three employees, may they know they are loved and matter.

On page 61 of *The Conscious Parent*, Shefali Tsabary writes, "To be a parent invites us to treat the reactions our children trigger in us as opportunities for spiritual growth." She explains that being triggered emotionally is an opportune time to stop, go inside, sit with it and deliberate on what the feelings are. This is being conscious. If being a parent is an ultimate trigger, going through the motions of losing a child is a prime opportunity to consciously examine love, loss, and the meanings life and death carry for us.

Even as I grieve, I know there is no death. I know Chloe will be well met, will be whole and will not suffer anymore. I know her journey continues, and this one will have brought her the experience she was looking for in her continuing journey to be all that she can be. I not only believe this—I know this.

On page 63, Tsabary speaks of embracing the "as is" moment. That is what I constantly say when referring to the life trajectory of Chloe. It is what it is. By accepting it, I can be there fully with her.

Solitude is critical to dealing with emotions. Simply sit with how it feels. There's no need to talk to anyone, get any advice or work anything out. Just sit with it. I call it burning logs. Just burn a few logs. Close the phone and sit. Staring at that fire (real or imagined) burns away a lot of confusion.

Time in palliative care means lots of time to wander halls, eat lukewarm food and think about death. You're basically living death all the time. Death becomes conscious, a fact of life. Here's a no-nonsense list of tips before you make that ultimate trip.

- Approach your death with no unresolved issues plaguing you. In a sense, go to sleep happy.

- Tidy up personal affairs.

- Make sure to throw away the written words you set down in your diaries when you were sad, bereft, heartsick or angry. Those words will be read and could create new, unresolved issues.

- Burn things that are over: old hurts, actions to forgive, people to forgive (including yourself), the past.

- Sit with the concept of death and talk to it. Make friends with it; know it as simply a stepping out of the body.

- Prepare well: write your instructions, prepare your own wishes and make conscious choices while you can.

My Diary: February 17, 2016

It's late afternoon, and you're in a semi-conscious state. I have no paper, so I use a paper towel from the bathroom to write upon. No worries. It's actually rough enough and thick enough to use as stationery. Not so great for hands though.

Your pulse is rapid, as if you're all geared up to exert yourself. You're fidgety, anxious and asking to be moved out of the room, to be strolled down the halls. Because your neck is weak, a wheelchair no longer suffices. I find one of those rolling chairs with a high back to support your head.

Someone hands me a booklet about the final stages of dying.

The process has certain typical signs. So this has happened before? We always think our situation is unique. It is anything but that.

Your chest rises rapidly. There's a pallor to your skin that makes it look as if the life inside you has already seeped out. Your eyes are rimmed in brown. I check your fingernails for telltale tints of blue. Your hands are lovely, perfect.

You're mumbling away, trying hard to stay conscious. You refused painkillers in order to try to stay sharp. "They make me too wobbly," you say.

The ordeal continues, yet by 8:00 p.m., with the help of some heavy drugs, you're sleeping. I go home to Mom's for the night. I have been with you all day. I want to stay, but because I've been there all day, your dad takes over, sleeping in the room.

At midnight, I awaken, feeling I should head to the hospital. I go. You're labouring to breathe. Your body is hot. I put my hands on you, speaking softly and saying all the things we think we would say at a moment like that. I say them all. I mean them all too. "I love you. The light is waiting for you. You are loved, everything is okay and it's time to let go."

Mom and Clo on a bicycle built for two - fall 2014

Your father is still asleep. I'm glad he doesn't wake up so I can have this intimate moment. You seem to calm down. I hope it's because my presence comforted you. That matters a lot to me. I slip out of the room and head upstairs to a lounge area to sleep. I'm not leaving. I can sense this is the end.

I awake at 2:30 a.m. as a wave, a tsunami of joy washes over me. At first, the emotion confuses me. My body aches. My back is killing me. I'm disoriented, and it takes a moment to register where I am. And yet I feel this incredible wave of joy. Then I realize it's over. You're free.

As your body becomes cold, I sit close to you, determined to memorize the physicality of you so that I can conjure you up in my mind in a day, a month or a decade from now. I feel you right there beside me. I tell you how courageous you are, how proud I am of you, how glad I am for you that you are now free.

You tell me how my calm demeanour helps you a lot. It's much harder for souls to make their way if we're all hysterical; they feel too guilty to move on. I tell you—no guilt. I recount the joy that washed over me. I still feel it. I associate your passing with joy and liberation and freedom. Part of me cries, and part of me rejoices.

I did commit the pattern of those freckles on your left forearm into my brain. I can picture them perfectly: a new constellation that brings consolation. I am a witness to a rite of passage that we all live. You have gone before me, perhaps an unnatural occurrence but a fact nonetheless. I am in awe.

I think of my father, still healthy at 89. Your passing gives my mother courage. It gives me courage too.

It is no longer the 17th. It's the early morning hours of the 18th. I stop for a moment and say thanks that you passed in the middle of the night. All is quiet and calm. I can sit with you uninterrupted, and I do so for almost two hours. No elevators, no chatter in the halls.

There's a silence about death that is necessary. There are no words to help one move through it. We simply do. Conscious living. Conscious parenting. Conscious dying.

CHAPTER 18

When Yes Means No

When yes means no. When no means yes. Paradox runs rampant through life. I chose entrepreneurship so that I could have more time with my children and the flexibility to run a business while raising three kids. Ha! There's a good reason it's called running and not walking a business. My life was a stoplight manicure. Flexibility was not part of the equation.

True stories. I sell my granola to an upscale hotel for their Sunday morning brunch buffet. When I call the chef on Monday, he tells me he absolutely won't reorder my product. Why? Because clients loved it too much. The cheaper fare went untouched, whereas the product I sent him was polished off. His food costs would be too high if he ordered my granola.

In another instance, a hotel received a whole pallet of free cereal from a competitor. Although he had loved my product, he couldn't pass up all that free product; it brought down his food costs. He stopped ordering from GEG. When yes means no.

The key was to not give up. When it got overwhelming, I went home, got under the covers and didn't talk to anyone. It would pass.

I like that line—it's called running a business, not walking a business. Life is a stoplight manicure. Where'd you get those lines?

From my head. They both came to me, and they mean the same thing essentially. The pace was relentless. I used to file my nails at the red lights. I had to use every precious second, and I was always running. I used to feel guilty for stopping long enough to sleep. There was always so much to do; it seemed self-indulgent to drift off at night.

That's nuts. I have an idea.

What's that?

I want to take those 12 chapter headings for GEG and relate them to my life. I might learn something about myself. Also, it might be fun to arrange the chaos in some kind of order.

Interesting concept. Like what I did with your 12 bridging steps.

How many left?

One. Tools.

Tools

Yes, I tried letting go of limiting beliefs. I practiced yoga and deliberate breathing. I projected love around boardroom tables and onto buyers, sellers and staff. Biographies of ordinary people doing extraordinary things helped to inspire me. I pictured myself with a Teflon skin that let problems slide off my back. I projected myself to 10,000 feet in my mind, in order to gain perspective on my small problems.

I also tried to learn from other leaders how to stay calm in a crisis and lead by example. But mostly I just winged it, guided by a pure intention, a strong why and Grandma.

Grandma taught me about patience and acceptance, about how my thoughts were creating my reality and there is no such thing as "end of life." There is only life after life. She still sounded the same, still had the same impatience and strength of character. She still had her sense of humour and could still get angry with me. She told me tangible things, affirmations to repeat that rang true to me and bolstered my confidence. Things like, "Andrea, every human soul is special and should be treated that way. All can be loved and nurtured. There is no exception to this basic rule of life."

And, "Repeat often: I am unique and valuable and have unlimited potential."

She asked me to translate that phrase into French, make cards and give them to anyone who would listen. Gradually, over the years of mentoring and lecturing in schools, I have offered the card as an affirmation that bolsters self-confidence. I still say it often, and it helps.

Grandma made her presence known in many ways, and she taught me many things. She still does. When I couldn't hear her voice clearly, there was always the nudge.

Follow the nudge: In a commercial kitchen, one always has to remove all jewellery. For this reason, I rarely went to work wearing jewellery of any kind. On this particular day, I had forgotten to remove my favourite earrings after having worn them the previous evening. Upon reaching the kitchen, off they came. Without thinking, I placed them in my locker rather than safely in a pocket.

When I came to leave that evening, I mistakenly dropped them and then kicked them under the employee lockers. They vanished.

Chastising myself, I decided to lift my spirits by stopping in unannounced at my parents' on my way home. Where else can you barge in without advanced warning and receive the warmest welcome and the biggest hugs? While driving there, I thought maybe it was time to treat myself to a new pair of earrings—a gold pair not like the costume jewellery I had just lost. I could finally afford them.

As I opened the door, my mother was standing there with a pair of earrings in her hand. "I have these for you," she said, handing me a lovely pair of 18-karat gold earrings. "I've had them in my drawer over 20 years. They were Grandma's."

I looked at her in amazement. Follow the nudge.

We are all guided, loved and protected by spirit. Call it what you will, this wisdom is constantly trying to help us follow our highest and best paths. They are constantly nudging us, and we are forever ignoring them. Imagine the patience it takes to never give up on us, to keep making that suggestion, repeating that warning or that inspirational thought, putting certain people on our path. The list is endless.

Our job is to follow the nudge. That nudge is the answer to all the asking we're doing. Listen for that nudge, and when you act on it, your angels rejoice.

That strong why, established in the business's infancy, guided me to know when to sell the business. As much as I lived and breathed this business, when it was done, it was done. The why had been fulfilled. The drive and motivation disappeared.

Okay, my turn. Here goes.

Why, Not How

What I get is that it's not about how I'm going to execute my plan—it's about why I want to do it in the first place. What is my intent? Why am I gonna get up in the morning, get out of bed early and go? So it's about what motivates me.

I never thought about it. I never thought about looking at the why of my choices. I thought about how a lot. How am I gonna find those drugs? How am I gonna find a place to sleep? How am I gonna get that nail polish?

Do you know that I stole about 36 bottles of nail polish in all? The funny thing is I almost never used them.

I couldn't look at the why. I was operating from "I want it. I'm having it." If I'd looked at the why, I would have been too discouraged. My motivation was crass, base and rudimentary. But it was so powerful that I couldn't stop. Right from the go, I'm already living in the subbasement. Great.

I can see why the why mattered for you. I had no idea. I took everything for granted. I'm so sorry.

Clo, it's way past the time to forgive yourself. Enough, now. All of life is one necessary loss after another.

Hmm …

Soup or Salad

This one's about knowing thyself. It too was off-limits to me. There was no introspection going on in this brain. There are so many great questions to ask the self: What am I chasing? What do I want? We all say we want to be happy, but what does that mean? What does happy look like to me? Happy now isn't happy five years from now. Also, I'm not who I was five years ago.

There are fundamentals that persist. By the way, did you know that your character pretty much stays the same through all your incarnations? Your likes and dislikes are mostly set. Your physical characteristics, your aptitudes.

In one life, you could be a singer. In the next, you won't have that talent, but you'll still love to sing. Achieving expertise sometimes takes several lives, so you keep working on the same skills, like a carver or a painter. Someone who sanded marble in one life can be a stone mason in the next.

Do you notice how all these big words are coming your way? Neuroplasticity, pigmentocracy, architectronics. I'm having a lot of fun dishing them out.

It did seem too coincidental to me.

It's no coincidence. There are no coincidences. There are only incidences that we engineer to coincide. You call it serendipity; we call it orchestration. So, here are the definitions.

Neuroplasticity describes how the brain can change across a life span. A person can do things that modify the functioning of the brain because of the existence of neuroplasticity.

Pigmentocracy is the ordering of society along colour lines, with whites at the top.

Architectronics describes how sounds make a composition, and how the same ideas that are used to inspire the composition of music can inspire architects.

Keep your eyes open, Mom. There's more to come. I like how you always have pen and paper ready. If you scribble it, you can scribe it later. The scribble and the scribe.

Nice.

Thought you might appreciate that. So, how was the death café last night?

It was my fifth death café. This one was, thankfully, just a half hour away from home—unlike the Peekskill adventure, which took over six hours to reach. We were seven people, the perfect number.

The facilitator had a gentle hand. I realize how important that is to the discussion. She made sure to include everyone yet didn't force anyone to speak.

I could feel her difficulty with acceptance of her daughter's death several years ago. Most of the discussion from others reflected their fears of being alone and of the unknown that restrict their actions while alive. Joanne was a good case in point. A good friend was dying. Rather than provide accompaniment and friendship, she pulled away due to her own fears of death. This made her feel guilty and bad about herself.

I also heard confusion. I would so much like to reassure

people that death is okay. Death is logical. Death is freedom and growth and moving forward. Death is so much more than that also. Death is life happening in its beauty and its pain. Death makes it possible to realize the importance of the present moment and to live life fully. Death makes it possible for the present moment to exist. One moment that is free of expectation.

You're so right about expectation, Clo. It is all about visualizing an outcome we can foresee and therefore is limiting. What if the plans collapse, the road is a dead-end and we're forced to veer away from our expected itinerary? We can end up receiving even greater gifts if we stop attaching expectation to an event.

The key is to move beyond expectation to allowing. Allow whatever presents itself. That matters not because the outcome could be so much less than we expect, but because it could be so much more. Thanks, Clo. You helped me learn a huge lesson.

So, I'm an awesome teacher! And you my willing student—or victim!

Back to soup or salad. I never saw myself before as a teacher. What are my likes? Now that I'm back in the land of heaven and honey, I get to clean up my act. While alive, I liked it grungy, second-hand, used and abused. That was just a role.

Next …

Bootstrapping

The next heading is bootstrapping—starting something out of nothing, picking yourself up by the seat of the pants or the edges of your boots and creating your life.

You could say that I bootstrapped my whole life, and you wouldn't be wrong. Do you remember the time I was taking a shower at the hospital? It was February. Minus 42 degrees outside. I had only my pyjamas, a towel and a bar of soap. I managed to deke out the orderly. Poor Tony. I know he got shit for that, but I had to go. I snuck out of the shower and helped myself to a coat and boots and a few dollars. Then off I went into the night.

I strolled out of there, AWOL. It was so easy. After a week with Gus, I couldn't stay with him a minute longer. He was too crazy. I was happy to go back to the hospital. The crazier people were on the outside, Mom. At least with the gang on the inside, they were medicated.

Bootstrapping was my life. I walked out of the hospital in Kenora, hitched a ride to Winnipeg and went looking for food. I hitched everywhere—seat of the pants, top of the boots, living on the cusp of nothing. Living on the street was mostly long and boring. And tiring, because you gotta keep walking. Then I met Wolf. That was a perfect name for him. Wolf was a drug dealer and pimp. He wore sheep's clothing, all right. I was too messed up to realize the hole I was in, and I kept digging. I mooched from everyone—no pride, no shame, no self. Just one thing in mind: survive.

The next one is the story of my life.

When No Means Yes

No matter what anyone said, I did exactly as I wanted. If I was chased out of a restaurant, I went in through the back kitchen door, helped myself and left. Rejection meant nothing. I had insulated myself from the scorn of others. It's like we both were pushed by rejection—me to be even more awful; you to turn a negative into a positive. Incredible.

How the same phrase can be interpreted in different ways!

Another gem today from Sue; she came over for lunch and met John. The three of us had lunch and a nice chat. She attributes this quote to Tony Robbins: "If you want to take the island, you gotta burn the boats." You've gotta commit.

The conversation was about growth and creativity, and how too much comfort stymies growth. Sue had a chat with a well-known artist in New York who was complaining that he had lost the inspiration to create. He was happy with his partner, and life was good. In other words, he was stuck.

When an artist reaches a place of domestic bliss, the art is doomed. A gut in turmoil is an environment rich for creativity. If the cookie jar's full, the easel is empty.

When no means yes—no to comfort, yes to the creative spark. The paradox of creating is that the less comfortable we are, the more we fight back, stimulating the spark.

Ultimately, science and spirituality will converge. So will the trajectory for the divine and the sublime, the light and dark, the sacred and the profane. The way there is fraught with obstacles, and the journey is so long that we don't realize the end game has been there all along.

At the Gym

At the gym implies learning from the obstacles. This doesn't apply to me. I learned nothing. I simply kept pushing until all of me broke down. I never strengthened a muscle, developed a strength. I dug myself a deeper and deeper hole. I was unable to see anything positive in what I was living. No gym membership for me.

I actually stuck around for you, not for me.

The next heading is hug and reward. It's about human-resource issues—hence hug and reward.

Hug and Reward

It's getting tougher to relate. Your world was all about creating something great, about using what you had both internally and externally. It was about motivating, pushing back against obstacles and appreciating the rejection.

When you're just surviving, you're hovering around the most basic needs of shelter, food and cigarettes. And not even in that order. The true order would be cigarettes, food and shelter. Nothing loftier, nothing more sublime than that. You're leeching, sucking dry, mooching, on the make, stealing with impunity, destroying your body and mind—and not bothered by whatever destruction you wreak around you. Think of the cost! It makes sense to take care of the down-and-outers because they cost society dearly.

I had no one to hug unless I count you, Daniel and Dad. I had no friends, no trust in others, no sense of community or collaboration. All those values disappeared when addiction and psychosis took over.

This is getting pretty grim. Let's try the next category.

Blame It on the Dopamine

Now this is something I can relate to. Drugs, meds, a chemical released in the brain that gives a person the energy to make it through a day.

Not funny.

I'll tell you something about addiction. We like to be with other addicts. Nothing much is demanded of us. No one wants us to change, to be fixed, to be different; we all accept each other as total losers. End of story. There's a certain comfort in being at the bottom and not even having to convince ourselves that it's okay to be there. And we have so much company! There's a lack of pretence.

Even with alternatives, with a loving family and great resources to lift me out of the mess, I loved the mess. I wallowed in it and was less stressed accepting my total defeat as a person rather than trying to lift myself out and have some expectation of a better life.

Almost every heading implies a state of mind diametrically opposed to mine. Take the next one.

Risky Business

It's about assessing risk and acknowledging the underlying assumption that each person's tolerance is different. It's as much about knowing thyself as "soup or salad" is, because it points out that no one knows our tolerance for risk like we do. No one can make our choices for us. So, know thyself and choose accordingly.

Or the next one.

I'll Be Faithful, I Promise

It's about integrity and giving your word and the written contract—again, ideals in a world I didn't inhabit. Was there a code of behaviour that governed my actions? Yes, a five-letter word: chaos.

All these ideals belong to the world of the creative, not the world of the destructive. To the builders and the visionaries and the doers, not the druggies and the pimps.

The Four Can Quota

And then there's my favourite one, the one about seeing the divine in the sublime, about Isaac and his cows and Mabou, Nova Scotia. It too descends into some kind of romantic fantasy about a simpler life, where all a man had to do was fill a certain quota each day.

Aided by his faithful cows, he filled that quota, trucked their milk to the dairy-processing plant, and then got on with his chores. Simple, predictable and blessed work.

In my world, no one works. We pilfer. We pollute. We're on the same planet, spinning in the same constellation, but our orbits are vastly different. Our world implodes constantly. People crash and burn from neglect, overdose and slow suicides assisted by Philip Morris and company.

I'd like to continue but can't relate to your headings. I do understand about tedium. Being homeless is tedious. Life is reduced to less and less as time goes on. A shedding of ego also ensues. That part was liberating.

Sometimes I imagined myself as the Buddha, just sitting for days under a tree in silent contemplation. But I was sitting in a drugged-out state of non-being.

We make pacts and agreements with our possessors. We pattern self-destruction into life. We weave decay. One great lesson I came to teach was the condition of unconditional love.

Mom, you were born into a very conditionally loving atmosphere. In order to be loved, you had to have the perfect grades, follow a certain path and offer up to the elders what they expected of you. Then you married a man whom was impossible to please no matter how hard you tried. No matter his actions, you were always characterized as being in the wrong.

You finally said, "Screw it. I can't make others happy." You realized how exhausting and impossible that was. The pressure to conform was so great, so constricting, that you finally let it go.

I came along and decided to break down every convention—exploring addiction, possession and an alternate life to the furthest degree. I tested you terribly. Daniel helped in this because he too wanted to beat his own drum. Once you started accepting him for who he is and not wanting him to be anything different, he moved a bit back towards the centre, going back to school and immersing himself in learning.

I lingered in palliative care for you so that you could gain experience and learn from others. I stayed around for you. I stayed suffering for you. The entity was ready to go, but I stayed just for you.

Was that cool or what, the way I woke you with a wave of bliss when I finally slipped out of that prison called my body?

You keep asking me what it feels like to have no body. Here is my lame attempt to describe it. It's like closing your eyes, hearing your favourite piece of music that touches your soul and feeling your heart soar high. It's like flying in your dreams, the mountain peaks tickling your belly as you skim by. It's like the moment the waterfall drops off the cliff—exhilarating. It's like the early morning sunrise across the water—silent. It's like having a really good pee when your bladder is super full—relief. It's like biting into a homemade chocolate chip cookie after it was frozen for a few minutes—delicious. It's like reaching your front door after trampling and struggling through knee-high snow—home.

Nice. Thanks for that, Clo. You've shined a light where before there was darkness. We haven't even discussed Socrates, Lincoln or the masses of topics that a lifetime touches on. We'll continue. I hope you'll stay a while.

I will. When it's time to go, you'll know.

Love you.

Love you.

CHAPTER 19

The righting moment is the best measure of a ship's overall stability. It describes the ship's true tendency to resist inclination and return to equilibrium. The righting moment is equal to the ship's righting arm multiplied by the ship's displacement.

Is this my righting moment, my moment when I resist being drawn into another person's drama and return to my true state of equilibrium?

Having no home untethers me. I don't have my own stuff, my own fortress of memories created from cherished moments. I have betrayal, heartache, grief and illness. I chose men who couldn't love me, who didn't appreciate me. They were not forced upon me.

You mean your writing moment?

Aren't you clever?

I'm clever and beautiful and all the things I wasn't in my life. I'm happy and productive, and I would like everyone to know that life really is beautiful. Just look at those rocks.

The rocks?

The inukshuk that your friend Carole made you. She has an eye for seeing life in rocks. She picks up rocks off the beach and turns them into friends, art and company, transforming rocks into characters. They take on personality and please us so much. Unstack them, and they're rocks. Stack them a certain way, and they take on a persona. Fascinating.

We do that with people too. It would be an interesting exercise to deconstruct, restack a slightly different way, change the perspective. And then the painted red heart grounds the image in a recognizable sentiment. It makes the inukshuk a benevolent friend. The power of a symbol.

My life was like a toppled inukshuk with the pieces put back together not quite perfectly. They were all there, just in the wrong order.

Nice metaphor, Clo.

The most amazing thing happened last night. I went to an evening of crystal bowls and sound at Carole's. I saw you cradling a baby and then launch the baby into the air. It became a million stars in the sky. I felt, about five times, this opening at the top of my head, this cylinder. I thought it was the horn of a unicorn or a vortex tunnel opening from my forehead. Then Lucille, who was sitting beside me, saw you. You actually told her your name. You asked her to thank me, and you said you placed a spark in my heart to comfort me in moments of sadness.

There is so much around me that comforts me in moments of sadness.

The ducks now appear right on my doorstep almost every morning, asking for food. Sometimes they come twice or three times in one day. The female eats first. Only when she's finished does the male approach. She ate from my hand this morning!

Mom, I never wanted to get old. I always thought I'd die young. Dying is simply living without the nuisance of shaving, showering and shampooing. It's life without body housekeeping. It's life without a body. No need to water the flowers—they're always glowing and growing. I have time to think, learn and grow.

Mom, you were looking at the trees this morning when you went out early. That was a sublime kayak ride, no? I was with you at one point. I tickled your nose.

I was wondering about that. All of a sudden, my nose began to itch. It was beautiful. The greens were brilliant and deep.

That's how they are here. All the beauty on the planet is magnified, and it transfixes me. Transfixation—another 13-letter beauty. It means "to be in a state of awe."

I just double-checked its meaning. It also refers to a surgical procedure done during an amputation.

A state of awe and an amputation—fascinating.

Where do you come up with those words?

Have you ever noticed what happens when you choose beauty?

What are you referring to?

I'm referring to conscious choice.

Being surrounded by beauty was a conscious choice. I just got back from an early morning kayak run. The lake was in a Zen state of calm. My mind became that way too. Ideas and themes to explore in my writing tumbled out as if the way had been cleared up.

It's amazing how much exercise a person can do when she isn't working 16 hours a day. I think about how I used to berate myself for not meditating or exercising. I barely had time to shower in the mornings.

I've uncovered another layer to my behaviour. Once I let go of needing, I switched to wanting. Now, I'm letting go of wanting. I'm wanting much less, and I'm doing more allowing. I'm not quite in a state of allowing, but I'm working on it. There's less clinginess and more space with John even though we're together a lot.

That's what's meant by being present. Allowing what is without wanting to modify it in any way. That's living in the now.

I was always a bit frustrated by trying to understand that phrase, "living in the now." I think I'm starting to understand it.

It's like what just happened to you.

What?

You spent the last 10 minutes looking everywhere for your sunglasses.

You're right. I did.

And what happened?

I finally realized they were on my head.

Exactly. Looking for beauty is the same thing. As is peace, perfection and well-being.

I got it. We go here and there. We look everywhere outside of ourselves when we really have everything within.

Bingo.

Rudimentary. Then again, what matters more than the rudiments of something? It lays the foundation for all other meanings that come later.

Like vestigial structures.

Gotta look that one up too. It means genetic structures that have lost most of their function as we have evolved—like the appendix.

Do you agree with that assessment?

You mean the idea that an appendix is now redundant?

Yes.

No. There is no part of the human body that is redundant.

Even our wisdom teeth? Did you know that babies are being born without wisdom teeth now?

They were important to process our diet millennia ago, but now that we have ways to make food less difficult to chew, we no longer need those large teeth.

So maybe there is something to the concept of vestigial structures? They are the blocks upon which the modern form rests. We can measure where we are from and where we were by assessing what structures are now vestigial.

Could we not extrapolate that there are vestigial structures in society and our cultural baggage?

Interesting concept. Like the idea of sin?

That's a good one. Like the idea that children should be seen and not heard. That the adults are the teachers, and children are the clean slates that need educating.

We could do a symbolic breaking down of vestigial structures—kind of like a burning of the vanities only without the self-flagellation and the scrapping of jewellery. There's no need to publicly burn books. Maybe we could do it kindly with gentleness, acknowledging that certain old ways of thinking don't serve us anymore. I like that.

Me too. Let's think about it. We could start a list.

Excellent idea.

Vestigial Structure #1: Children need us, the wise adults, to form their minds.

Let's call them VSs, okay?

Okay.

VS #2: It's really important that everyone like me. To avoid controversy, I play a role and cover up my true self so that others see only the agreeable, pleasant, compliant, perfect me.

VS #3: The world is a place of scarcity.

I actually thought that if I didn't marry your dad, no other man would ever love me. Scarcity thinking. This was deeply entrenched in me. Yet abundance is all around me.

I'm feeling sad today. It's Father's Day. I've spent my birthday, Christmas and New Year's Eve alone. I'm no stranger to being alone. It simply makes me reflect on family and on how ours disintegrated. I despise myself when I go into self-pity mode.

Did you like that word I popped into your brain in the car?

I completely forgot about it. You mean gloominosity?

Yup.

I just looked it up. It means "light reflected off dirty and wet city streets." Bizarre. Where do you come up with these words?

I'm impressed that you actually picked that one up right away.

The funny thing is I don't doubt you for a second. It's me I have doubts about. Is my writing good enough? Should I be going about this a different way?

Stop the self-slander. Stop. Just stop.

It's hard to stop those negative thoughts. Okay, enough. Just keep writing, AC.

Lean on me, Mom.

As in lean on you, or be lean on you?

Words, words. Nothing is as much fun to manipulate. To love words is to love the possibilities of endless combinations of letters and to create endless worlds of thought. Thought is everything here. We think, and we are. The speed of that takes getting used to. The lightness of being takes getting used to.

Mom, as an aside, healing circles are powerful. When you attend the Tuesday night sound healing at Carole's, please direct your healing with intent, not just a general, all-over-the place idea of sending healing. Send it to a specific person or a specific spot on the planet, or even to a specific vibrational frequency. Get specific with your healing thoughts, and they'll have much greater value and volume.

More alliteration—vibration, value, volume.

It's like we're not only writing this story but are in it as well. As if it's being written while we write. The actors, the writers, the directors, the extras, the make-up and the costume designers—we're the cast.

The word cast: an ensemble of people whose goal is to put on a show; a hard casing designed to properly set a broken bone; to toss away as in cast aside or cast out; a castaway: one who is cast out of safe harbour into the unknown.

All those meanings from one four-letter word. There's another four-letter word that fascinates us. How could four little letters prove to be so effective in pissing off so many?

It describes a loving act as well as an unloving one. It's a verb, a noun, an adverb and the adjective of choice. Not only is someone an idiot, but they're an effing idiot. Said out loud or muttered to oneself, it's our go-to word.

It's just four letters, people. Relax.

It's 4:45 a.m. I'm up after having an interesting dream I want to record. I'm in the house up north. I wake up in the morning to find that the house was completely turned around by a severe storm during the night. It is now literally balancing on the edge of a cliff, precariously close to the abyss. Before getting out of there quickly, I grab two pairs of eyeglasses. Nothing else. One is an old frame I used to wear that no longer is my correct prescription. The other is my glasses for writing.

I interpret it to mean that my life has turned around completely and is now different than it was. I can no longer look at it through an old lens or with old beliefs and values. The past is over. I should forget everything else and just write.

Chapter 20

Desert, oasis, desert, oasis. Life is like that. We flounder, we falter and we search. The struggle threatens to engulf us. Then we have some clarity, a moment of peace while we walk the beach. Then it's back to the struggle of the desert. Searching, questioning, wondering what is the meaning of this madness. We work to get out of that discomfort zone and eventually move towards another oasis. We arrive and thrive, and then growth creates more challenge. And on and on it goes. A new acronym for life: DODO.

My lovely cottage - fall 2016

Happy, like Monday-morning seagulls after the Sunday picnickers have left.

Thank you for taking the nudge and trusting it. By typing with your eyes closed, we can connect anywhere, even in a busy airport. We don't like to talk to you in such busy places. There's too much commotion, too many thoughts, too may souls, too much activity and movement to be able to tune in properly. Yet it still works. Keep doing it this way, and you'll see the connection gets even stronger and clearer.

Clo, I didn't make one mistake in the above paragraph. That's a small miracle in itself. I closed my eyes and wrote slowly.

So finally, after four months of writing, we've created a tactic that will speed this along incredibly. A cool oxymoron. You know how I love oxymorons. By typing slower, you speed up the process. You create greater connectivity to me. Type slower, go deeper and connect faster. What do you feel in your hands?

They are vibrating. All of me is vibrating this morning. I really love this idea of typing with my eyes closed. It further teaches me to trust. I'm making fewer errors than with my eyes open.

Notice how this vibe of happiness is contagious with John. If a person presents herself as illuminated, as fulfilled and happy, she will attract the like. Present yourself as you are.

The funny thing is I am making more mistakes with my eyes open than closed, because I type so much faster. Typing with my eyes closed is an exercise in trust as well. Trust the touch. Trust that my grade eight typing teacher, Mr. Davies, did a great job. Thank you, Mr. Davies. All these years later, I acknowledge you. You didn't feel very acknowledged in your life. My role, which comes to me more and more each day, is to acknowledge people, to see them, to let them know how they are special and that they are loved. They often forget that fact in the hustle of life on earth.

All love is love. There are no degrees of love, just circumstances that open or close the heart. All love is love. The love for a pet is often purer than the love towards a parent. We have put a shroud of guilt around that by judging ourselves as imperfect or impure when we love our pets and eventually grieve our pets more than our family members. The greater the unconditional nature of the love, the more one will grieve. So don't make your love wrong.

Simply love John as you do—nothing more, nothing less. Don't shorten the cycle of this experience because you may judge it as less than a perfect love. It is love, and therefore it is perfect. I just forgot how to spell the word therefore. *How bizarre is that? For a moment, my love for you so overwhelmed me that my flow of logic was interrupted by emotion. I lost my cool.*

How blessed is that! Je t'aime, Cherie.

Moi aussi, Maman.

In answer to your question, the reason you can hear me and all spirits easier at 35,000 feet is because the density of consciousness is much less than on the ground. There are fewer souls around you. This concept has many interesting repercussions on earth.

There is a need to hear spirit. Spirit is much easier to hear when the density of thought around you has lessened—less people, less density of thought. Getting off the ground is, in fact, a way to know God. As is getting out of densely populated areas. Malls, airports, movie theatres, stadiums—all have a high density per square foot. Make sure to get to a place of space as often as you can.

You are surrounded by water. Get out on the water as often as life permits.

Am I talking to Chloe? This feels different.

You're now talking with her oversoul. The tone has become more formal. We can do this because you are up in the air, en route. This has been a welcomed side effect of man taking to the air, whether by hang glider, supersonic jet, or commercial aircraft. You might extrapolate that the thinner the air, the thinner the interference to this communication. It is a blessed moment, no?

It also helps me understand why I always loved to fly. I'm closer to spirit.

Precisely.

Hi, Clo. You're back.

Yup.

Let's work this new method. I take dictation and type with my eyes closed while listening to chakra-clearing Zen music.

Precisely.

Now you sound like your oversoul.

I am one with my oversoul. Like an onion, Chloe is simply one of the outer layers.

I am human and divine. I am therefore filled with paradox and self-doubt and conflicting thoughts and impulses. One thing I don't doubt is you. One thing I do doubt is me.

Did you ever doubt your capacity to love me?

I doubted my capacity to tolerate you, to be able to accept your life without judging it, to love you in spite of yourself.

And in the end?

In the end, we made total peace with each other. It was blessed and beautiful and perfect. It was grace and divine, and when it was done, all was well.

So follow your heart, and all will be well. Do you love this man?

I have nothing but love for him. For all his life experience, he's still a kid: enthusiastic, fun and passionate.

There's room in my heart for everyone, Clo. Even your dad

and your grandmother. I can only send them love. I feel myself vibrating with love. I am love.

Anything worthwhile takes effort. We're going to break down the word effort.

E is for the energy that will gather to assist you.

F is for Friday. Keep one day a week aside for this work. One whole day so that you can be silent, turn off the phone, drink a lot of water, stay home and do the work. The work may be meditating on and off all day. It may include exercising, writing, chanting, dancing, singing or gardening. Whatever it is, it is one day a week devoted to your higher self.

F is for friendships. Choose only the ones that nurture you.

O is for orgasm. Yup. Remember to honour the physical self, and then as you do, watch what happens. You will attain orgasms of a magnitude you've never experienced just by communicating with spirit. Your body begins to transcend the physical. Note it. Be aware of it. Enjoy it. They begin as goosebumps, but hang on, and they will intensify.

R is for repeat, repeat, repeat. That needs no explanation.

T is for take time to teach. In so doing, you will learn.

EFFORT.

One of the immediate rewards of writing is that you realize when the words are yours and when they are not. When it's you, it's more work. When it's from beyond, you simply have to present yourself.

When you took the 12 steps, you weren't drinking enough water. Also, your grief was still recent and raw. As you integrate loss with gain, two sides of the same coin, you're able to be more objective.

Clo, sometimes I feel so close to John, and sometimes I feel like there's a basic incompatibility in our energy. Do you concur?

Yes. Here is the irony. If you don't advance your psychic skills, you can remain very happy with John. However, if you do that, you'll eventually be unhappy, because you'll be denying your true self to yourself. If you do continue on this road of developing your abilities, of meditation, of authenticity and of expansion, then you may grow apart as your energy becomes incompatible. This doesn't mean you won't always love each other. You will. You will remain close friends. Trust that what is most appropriate will present itself.

So, once again, it's about what do I have to learn from this relationship?

Be grateful for the healing you received. Know that your request to live surrounded by beauty was heard and fulfilled. That remains such a strong desire for you that you will always be drawn to fulfil it no matter where you live.

Learn that each must evolve. Each must grow. He has pushed you to non-response, to non-reactivity. That was part of the role he's played. You could only learn that when faced with situations you would normally react to (i.e., feel offense, pack your bags; or feel alarmed, pack your bags; or feel slighted, pack your bags; or feel uncomfortable, pack your bags). For you, the result of reactivity has been the same: pack your bags. It may have been pack your bags to leave the relationship (as you did with Isi) or pack your bags and take off on a solo trip (as you also did when you were with Isi). You need to call him.

Who? Isi? Why?

To acknowledge to yourself that you've learned what you needed to learn, and now you're totally over him. Over.

How about I meditate on it?

Before you meet your soul mate, you have to know your soul. How else would you recognize the mate to that energy if you aren't conscious of the energy yourself? You would not be able to recognize him. Most people marry long before they know their own souls. Then as they begin to awaken to who they are, they realize they chose the wrong mates. There is a basic timing problem.

Procreation must ignite through young bodies. However, awareness of self, for past generations, happens only in the fifth or sixth decade. Incompatible timing, no?

The new ones entering your realm have no such lapse or drag in awareness. They are born with awareness and therefore will choose their partners with awareness and procreate with awareness, ensuring energy compatibility from a young age. This will improve family life, result in fewer divorces and create a society with a strong fabric of interdependence and less rupture. We see the positives already in evidence through the work written on indigo children. This is evolution during your lifetime that you can measure. The planet is evolving!

Thank you. Clo, you there?

Yup.

I'm heading to England tomorrow for a course in Trance Mediumship. What do you think?

It's about fucking time!

Now that sounds like the Clo I know and love!

Funny, funny. Notice how the phone is not ringing.

Yup. I have the space to write without interruption.

This is what you need. You need uninterrupted time. You need to be on your own. Watch: this will be corroborated by others. Please listen!

I will. Sometimes I don't listen well. I hear, but I don't listen. I lack courage. Please help me have the courage to hear, to listen and to choose wisely.

Do you notice how you need time to edit and time to write? It is the same with life. One needs time to go over past experience, assimilate and unpack it even as one moves eagerly into new experiences with all the spontaneity and adventure that brings. Be one with all of it—the messy memories, the pain and the unknown joys still ahead.

I'm sad tonight. I have the tube of Caudalie facial mask here beside my computer as I write. It's actually called an instant detox mask. Impossible to look at the packaging and not think of those facials in the hospital. I'm looking out my window onto the moon's reflection across the water, and I'm sad because I have to share what I know with John. He's opening his heart to me.

Sometimes you have to let go what you love. Do you not see how perfect is this plan?

Perfect? It feels painful. More loss.

New projects on the horizon. New excitement to fuel your growth and keep pushing you forward.

I did something symbolic last night, but I'm not sure you got the meaning.

Are you talking about when you came to me upside down? I actually saw your face upside down.

Yup.

That did seem a bit strange. I think I get it, but tell me the reason.

It was a symbol of the possibility to appear in ways you don't normally associate with me. There is logic in the logic-defying vision of an upside-down Chloe. Appearing to you upside down was my way of defying logic to help you remember that I will appear in different ways. You can still call me Chloe for as long as you like, but you realize that is simply a small part of this oversoul.

Now I feel both dazed and disturbed by that. So Chloe no longer exists as she did?

No. Not only is the physical manifestation of her now simply ashes and dust, but the personality is melding back into the whole soul, or oversoul. I will sound less and less like Chloe and more and more like the total being that comprises the personality Chloe, as well as all the other personalities of all the incarnations I experienced in human and other forms.

Now I really feel like I'm losing her.

That also contributed to your melancholy over the last three days.

I didn't think there was a way to explain that feeling. It was deep and sad, and it kept me on the verge of tears.

The challenge is not much different than the one you take upon yourselves when relating to another in physical form. Can you see them as multifaceted? Can you see them as having the divine within? Can you see them as so much more than you see?

Will you still remember everything about the time you were Chloe?

Everything.

Will we still be connected?

We were, are and will always be connected. However, the relationship is changing because we resolved many concepts in this previous lifetime. Dependence, independence, conditional and unconditional love, expectation, acceptance and finally allowing, opening the energetic shift towards death as a more understood part of life.

We've been busy.

By explaining this shift, I hope to allow for your conclusion that sharing this information is the logical outgrowth of so much heartache on your part. When you agreed to return that snowy night in December 1991, you were taking on another contract that has taken these many years and many tears to fulfil.

To be a mouthpiece for the dead is a blessed role. Not for the faint of heart or the indecisive.

That snowy night in February years ago, driving through the vast, wintery blizzard between Winnipeg and Kenora to rescue your daughter, was not for the meek either. Visiting her in the psych ward, and finding the patience and compassion to accompany her over more than a dozen admittances. The multiple injustices, management and recovery from physical pain, allowing without reacting to the criticism and judgement of others, the absence of a partner, the challenge of creating financial independence, founding and running a business ethically and successfully, spending her last year together with Daniel, a family at last—none of this is for naught.

It has all created the sum total of the personality called Andrea.

My tone is changing. It is becoming less personal, less the voice of your child. Now you understand why we often do not reconnect with loved ones, because as we evolve back into our higher selves, that one distinct personality from that one incarnation melts back into the whole being.

By continuing the conversation as we have done, you grieve anew every day. This too is difficult. However, your understanding that there is simply life after life makes the process liveable for you. It also provides the opportunity for you, as for so many others, to give voice to the dead.

Hear us. Rejoice for us. Love us. Remember us. And one day, join us.

Clo, can I talk to you, please? I'm not quite ready for this.

Hi, Mom. Breathe. I'm as close as your nose, remember? Have you ever spent a moment, eyes closed, breathing into the centre of a rose? Try it, and know how eternity feels. It's that simple. All these great complexities simply come down to knowing we are part of eternity, we never die and all is love.

You're fierce, Mom. Thanks for this. Thanks for everything.

I love you, Clo.

Made in United States
North Haven, CT
14 April 2024